THE
ALIGNED
HUMAN

THE ALIGNED HUMAN

Finding Balance in an Ever-Changing World

SMITA SHANKAR

ISBN: 979-8-89694-730-1 - Ebook

ISBN: 979-8-89694-731-8 - Paperback

ISBN: 979-8-89694-732-5 - Hardcover

Get the free journal here:

To get the best experience with this book, I've found readers who download and use The Well-being Pyramid Journaling Workbook greatly benefit from the physical act of writing on printed paper for a deeper connection to one's thoughts through the tactile process of hand writing. Enjoy!

author.smitashankar.com/bk/journal

To my girls, Sejal and Devika, for always encouraging me to put my words out there. You show me every day what it is to be courageous and authentic.

Acknowledgements

*To all who care about well-being and want better—
for themselves, humanity, and the planet.*

Table of Contents

Introduction 1

Chapter 1 The Well-being Pyramid 11

Part 1

Chapter 2 What Drives Us? 23

Chapter 3 Mind Traps...37

Chapter 4 The "Optimized" Mind 49

Chapter 5 Nourishment of the Mind 63

Part 2

Chapter 6 Body Metaphors...75

Chapter 7 Holistic Body as Interconnected Systems......83

Chapter 8 Nourishment of the Body............................91

Part 3

Chapter 9 Belief Systems, Spirit, Soul 111

Chapter 10 Your Authentic Self 119

Chapter 11 Nourishment of the Soul............................127

Part 4

Chapter 12 Triggers and Environmental Toxicity.......... 141

Chapter 13 Space as a Mental Construct 155

Chapter 14 Nourishment of Space 163

Part 5: Dual Dynamics of the Well-being Pyramid

Chapter 15 Disconnect of Mind and Body 173

Chapter 16 The Heart of the Mind.............................. 189

Chapter 17 The Mind's Perception of Space and Time.. 197

Chapter 18 Accessing Spirit through the Body.............207

Chapter 19 Choreography of Body and Space 215

Chapter 20 Qualia and Consciousness..........................223

Part 6: Ahead

Chapter 21 The Precious Choice in Every Moment.......237

Introduction

The metamorphosis of caterpillar to butterfly is some next-level alien magic. The caterpillar's sole purpose is to eat and grow. It cannot reproduce or continue on a cycle of life. Imagine if it were aware and knew it was just a matter of time before it would encase itself in a self-made cocoon, its tissues breaking down as the body restructures into the legs, wings, antennae, and other body parts that make up a butterfly.

What if we humans experienced such a metamorphosis? Would our caterpillar dreams be an anticipation of the coming freedom of flight? Would we ritualize the process? Regard it as a rite of passage? Would it be a heady mixture of pain and joy, not unlike childbirth? Perhaps we would rename our butterfly selves, putting to rest our former caterpillar appellations.

We metamorphose—from infant to child, to adolescent, to adult, and finally to an elder, should we be blessed with a long life. Metamorphosis is a series of gradual transitions and much more complex in humans—after all, we have our mental, physical, emotional, and spiritual selves with which to contend. Whether all, few, or none of these areas transform at any stage is unique to the individual. Universally, we are meant to reconstruct, evolve, "grow wings," and soar. That is life. It's what we celebrate in others and what our hearts truly yearn for.

Life is very often so hard. We may feel we are victims of our special circumstances and that life is an endless stream of suffering. We may become distracted and prioritize some choices above all others, such as wealth, status, and power. We may be so prone to perfectionism that we become crippled with indecision. We may be traumatized by an event and find ourselves living with excessive caution. We may be so controlled by our rage that we alienate ourselves from love. In these moments, our past may seem to be dictating our future, limiting the possibilities available to us. Yet, our lives are not set in stone.

There are infinite possibilities for how our lives may unfold. How do we choose to observe ourselves, course-correct, and align for health, abundance, and well-being, and in doing so evolve to become better versions of ourselves? That is the central question of this book. In answering that question, the *Aligned Human* metamorphosed from an idea to the framework for true well-being you are about to learn.

To get to this point, I grappled with the question of what it means to be aligned, how the mind, body, spirit, and space are key components that must be in balance to be an aligned human. Alignment helps us to become better versions of ourselves. It creates the necessary scaffolding for moving toward authentic well-being and conscious growth. The growth in consciousness is essential to understanding your life from a higher vantage point, above the issues and challenges of everyday life, with a wisdom that comes from having a wider lens, a larger, more encompassing perspective of who you are as an individual and as a member of the human collective.

As spiritual author and speaker Wayne Dyer wisely said, *"Change the way you look at things, and the things you look at change."* Your life will be as joyous, abundant, and meaningful as you choose to view it and live it. Every life event is an opportunity to evolve, become more, and become wiser. Every decision that leads to suffering is just as informative to the self-reflective person as the decisions that lead to desired outcomes.

Your own life journey has been gifted to you—complete with everything you need to improve, transcend limitations, and learn. Through observation, introspection, and inspired action, you may realize the extraordinary nature of your existence. You are the only you that has ever lived or ever will be.

When I was about a year and a half old, my parents took a picture of me as I was wandering around our expansive backyard in Hyderabad, India, with a small branch in one hand and a doll in the other. What struck me was how tranquil, present, and joyful I looked. I seemed to be at peace within and with the surrounding nature. Was I imagining it, or did my face glow as if lit from within?

Some time ago, at one of my most difficult moments, I saw this picture and asked myself: Where did she go and how do I get back to her? Then, years of struggle, pain, chronic illness, squashing my spiritual inclinations, and compromising my authentic self in favor of what I thought was a more successful version of myself had taken its toll. Well-being seemed an elusive possibility for so long.

It has been a long journey from head to heart and a deeply introspective one. I had to define and understand well-being for myself, and the result of that is a framework for well-being that has served me well and can be utilized by anyone to achieve holistic alignment in their lives.

Have you been searching through your life for a nonspecific, intangible something that would counter the anxiousness, emptiness, and loneliness that lies beyond languor or ennui? Whether you attribute it to external circumstances in your life or you struggle to rationalize the feelings at all, that deep sense that something is missing is your call to step back and pause before you do anything to damp down or address any uncomfortable feelings that arise.

Whether you call it your Higher Self, God, the Universe, Gaia, or something else, this energy that vibrates at a high frequency is at every moment reaching out to you, asking to co-create with you the unfolding that is your life. Choose here and now to embrace that co-conspirator, and see every moment as a lesson in Earth school. Consciously become a student of the Universe, and you'll be surprised by the support you receive. You are never alone. Even in the most soul-crushing, devastating circumstances, the Universe, in its infinite wisdom and compassion, wants for you the expansion of consciousness and authentic well-being. So it provides a mirror into which you may gaze and truly know yourself. That mirror is your life, and that can inform you greatly on your life path and quest for well-being.

What is well-being, really?

Well-being is intrinsic to human health and a healthy lifespan. By definition, there is a holistic nature to well-being. It alludes to an overall quality of life that includes, but is not limited to, physical and mental health. Well-being encompasses the emotional, social, and spiritual dimensions. Most of us know something about wellness, and we want that—the intangible Holy Grail of complete well-being. We want to enjoy life more, worry and struggle less, and experience more love. We want a long and healthy life, a healthspan, and not just a lifespan. According to a May 17, 2024, article in Science Daily, we are living longer lives but spending more time in poor health.[1] How can one be an exception to that trend?

Health, as defined by the World Health Organization (WHO), is "a state of complete physical, mental, and social well-being and not merely the absence of disease or infirmity." So how is the overall health of humans on this planet? World health statistics for 2024 indicate we were on a steady global upward trend of life expectancy and healthy life expectancy (HALE) until the 2020 pandemic. Life expectancy rose from 66.8 years in 2000 to 73.1 years in 2019, and HALE increased from 58.1 years to 63.5 years in 2019, according to the WHO. Post-pandemic, life expectancy dropped to 71.4 years in 2021, and HALE fell to 61.9 years in 2021.[2] Clearly, something is amiss in our efforts to thrive.

The Global Wellness Institute defines wellness as the active pursuit of activities, choices, and lifestyles that lead to a state of holistic health.[3] Their website lists the multi-dimensional aspects of holistic health as: physical, mental, emotional, spiritual, social, and environmental. This shows that wellness is not an end goal but a lifelong journey. Later on, I'll share with you my life-changing journey with devastating ill health that fueled my desire to seek holistic well-being and thrive, rather than just survive, which served as the impetus for the creation of this book, *The Aligned Human*.

Central to the *Aligned Human* is a three-dimensional conceptual framework called the Well-being Pyramid (WP), representing an individual's well-being. My journey through illness highlighted for me a larger truth: holistic well-being is the interplay of the dimensions of mind, body, spirit, and space. This realization forms the basis of the Well-being Pyramid—a framework to guide you through life and the impending changes that are inevitably en route and will shake up life as we have known it. Much of that is already underway, as we can see through devastating weather events, industry disruption due to generative AI, rising incidences of complex chronic issues like autoimmune diseases, and political upheaval. I demonstrate through the book how to apply the WP so that it may serve as a framework for you in your life.

The key element of the WP is you—as the human awareness independent of mind, body, soul, and space. Draw a line from the pinnacle of the pyramid down to the center of the base. That is your axis of consciousness. You, as awareness, are a point on this vertical axis at your current level of consciousness. The closer you reside to the pinnacle, the higher your consciousness (see Figure 1). Chapter 1 describes the WP in greater detail, further defining one's expansion in consciousness as it is represented in the WP.

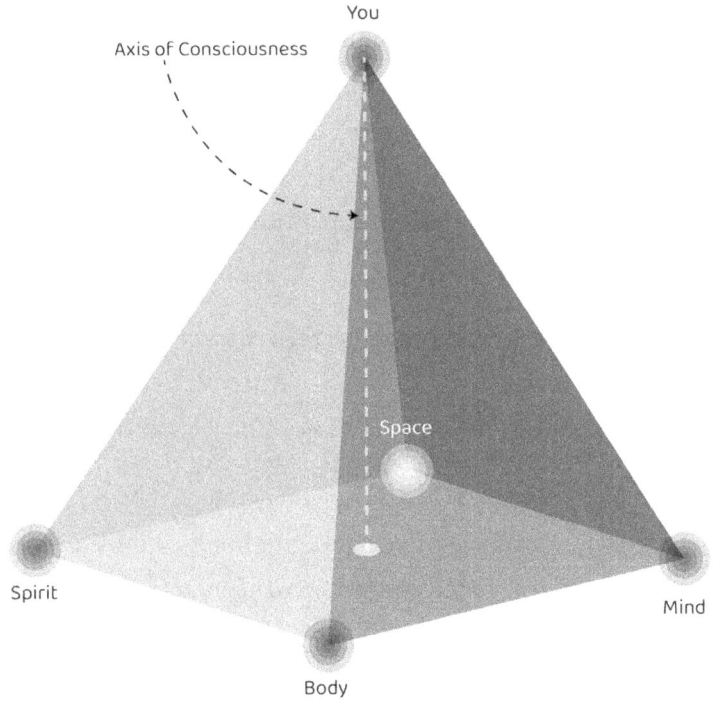

Figure 1 The Well-being Pyramid

The journey to a more conscious world is one we have all been called to undertake. You can own your well-being, become a more conscious human, and a true custodian of the planet. Your effort impacts all beings around you and the whole world because we are all connected. This shifts the collective.

Human alignment is representative of the degree of balance and equanimity within you, as well as your alignment with everything outside your self-determined boundaries, both physical and nonphysical.

A high level of attunement can ensure that you engage with your external world with openness, compassion, and reverence, and is key to ultimately expanding individual and collective human consciousness. The ultimate goal of human alignment is wisdom—and higher consciousness is foundational to that. We must bring wisdom into everything we do—the technology we develop, our relationship with ourselves, each other, and the planet.

This book discusses wisdom in the final chapter: what it is, why it is so vital, particularly in this age of artificial intelligence, and what might be possible for us as a global collective of wise humans.

Thank you for choosing to explore this book, and I sincerely hope it aids you on your journey toward alignment, well-being, and the authentic You. My other wish is that you realize that you must be an active participant in your personal future and our collective future, as the choices humanity makes now will have far-reaching effects on our well-being. It will shape every one of our futures as well as those of our descendants for lifetimes to come.

Through your commitment to owning your well-being and your willingness to leverage your life experiences as points of learning, you will feel a deeper connection to self, peace, equanimity, and a path forward and upward to higher consciousness and wisdom.

I assure you, life will get better—so much better. You will learn through the *Aligned Human* how to ride the wave of life and thrive, transcend present circumstances, find authentic well-being, and be a transformative soul guide to others on their journeys through life.

Throughout the book, I mention new and evolving powerful technology like artificial intelligence. How we choose to develop and incorporate these technologies can either catapult the planet to a new era of abundance and well-being or lead us to deterioration. So the core message of this book is urgent. We have a world in flux, changing rapidly, with many events that seem threatening and maddening, causing great despair. AI is inevitable and instrumental as a tremendous facilitator of change for the planet. This is a time for enlightened, heart-centered individuals to step up and be full participants in humanity's choices.

So I hope you read the book, understand the Well-being Pyramid, and make it your own: tailor it to your life, your challenges, and circumstances. Help yourself so that you may have the wisdom and energetic fortitude to help others. Above all, never, ever give up!

The Well-being Pyramid

"Most persons are so absorbed in the contemplation of the outside world that they are wholly oblivious to what is passing on within themselves."

NIKOLA TESLA, MY INVENTIONS: THE AUTOBIOGRAPHY OF NIKOLA TESLA

The pyramids have fascinated me since I was a child and had the opportunity to visit Giza, on the outskirts of Cairo, Egypt. Oblivious to the dry desert heat and shielding my eyes, I squinted up at the Great Pyramid with absolute wonder and fascination. Even then, I knew something was very special about this space and those structures. The pyramid as a symbol for human well-being is intriguing to me and was the inspiration for this book's metaphor of a pyramid that represents the dynamics that influence and impact each of us throughout life.

In ancient times, the pyramid represented the earth at the base, with its pinnacle pointing to the sky or heaven. Considered a powerful and sacred symbol, it represents the soul's journey from life to afterlife, from earth to heaven. The pyramid also represents one's spiritual evolution or ascension to higher consciousness. The two-dimensional view of the pyramid is a triangle, which symbolizes strength. The number three is symbolic of the phases of life (birth, life, death) or the three realms of Heaven, Hell, and Earth.

For Nikola Tesla, a Serbian-American engineer, futurist, and inventor, the pyramids were a lifelong obsession. He believed that the pyramids were a power plant, able to generate and transmit electricity; they even inspired his experimentation with the wireless transmission of energy, long before the technology was available and used as it is today. Tesla was a visionary well ahead of his time when he imagined transmission towers that could be dispersed geographically to transmit power over long distances.

As the ancient pyramids are thought to be an energetic source of power, we humans are energetic beings too. If we can hone and harness our own power from within, we can be our own sources of energy, well-being, and forces for positive change. The Well-being Pyramid is a conceptual model that represents the components of your well-being and your relationship with them.

The four points on the square base of the Well-being Pyramid are mind, body, spirit, and space. Your relationship to these components forms the framework of your mental, embodied, spiritual, and spatial well-being. There is much to describe in each of these areas that will illustrate for you the holistic nature of well-being, and perhaps provide insight that will aid you in your own quest toward total health.

As I mentioned in the Introduction, the axis of consciousness on the WP provides a way to understand levels of consciousness and the progression toward more expanded awareness. Richard Barrett, an author and thought leader, outlined seven levels of consciousness corresponding to one's stage of development:

Level 1 Survival - Meeting basic needs for food, shelter, and health

Level 2 Conforming (Relationships) - Safety, family, friendship, belonging

Level 3 Differentiating (Self-Esteem) - Security, confidence, positive self-image, recognition

Level 4 Individuating (Transformation) - Freedom, autonomy, accountability, courage, personal growth

Level 5 Self-Actualizing (Internal Cohesion) - Honesty, trust, creativity, authenticity, meaning, internal alignment

Level 6 Integrating (Making a Difference) - Collaboration, empathy, intuition, mentoring

Level 7 Service - Compassion, forgiveness, humility, contribution, future generations [1]

At level 1, you simply want to survive. You may have limiting beliefs about your ability to control your circumstances. At level 4, you are interested in discovering who you are beyond familial, societal, and cultural influences. At level 7, your work is your purpose, and your goals are about making a difference for others. It is marked by selfless service.

So, the levels of consciousness ascend the WP axis of consciousness.

Our current economic systems are mostly based on level 1 survival—consumption and immediate gratification. However, if we are indeed moving toward higher consciousness as a human collective, it stands to reason that the legacy structures and institutions we continue to support today for our economic, healthcare, educational, and other systems are crumbling and transitioning to more collaborative, equitable, and sustainable frameworks that will better reflect and serve our consciously evolving human collective. Perhaps you've been sensing these changes and the seismic shift that is coming to how we manage our lives.

Per Barrett, these stages of consciousness coincide with stages of development of a human from birth to end of life. However, if you encounter trauma or other adverse conditions, (and let's face it, historically the world we have built has always provided ample threats to our lives, our culture, our sense of security) it will be challenging to naturally progress toward higher stages of consciousness as you develop and mature from childhood to adulthood and to the final years without resolving those traumas.

Another model for stages of development/consciousness was presented by Abraham Maslow, an American psychologist who helped develop the humanistic psychology theories.[2] He identified a hierarchy of human needs in the 1950s.[3] According to Maslow, humans require the fundamental basics of food, water, shelter, air, sleep, clothing, and reproduction at minimum. Once those needs are met, safety, security, and employment fill out the next level of need. Stacked on top of that are the psychological needs of love and belonging. The top level on the stack concerns growth and fulfillment, or self-actualization.

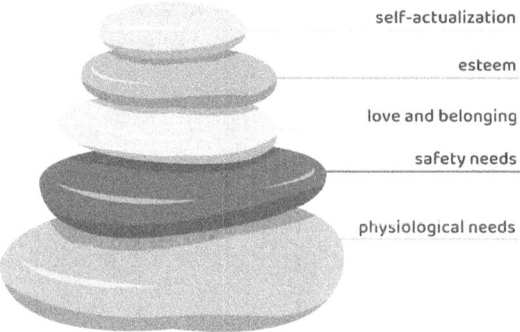

self-actualization

esteem

love and belonging

safety needs

physiological needs

Figure 2 Maslow's Hierarchy of Human Needs

Since the introduction of Maslow's hierarchical pyramid, other psychologists have sought to modify the theory. Issues of cultural and situational context have been brought forth to demonstrate that human needs are dependent on the social constructs of the culture to which they belong, and may not follow a neat stacking of levels at all.

Maslow believed in a stage beyond self-actualization, which he wrote about in his personal notes. Unfortunately he died before being able to publish this concept. He called it self-transcendence, which extends to motivations and causes beyond one's self, often characterized by selfless acts of service. At this level, one has broken free of societal, cultural, or religious identities, and grown beyond individualism or culture to a "sense of purpose anchored in the plight of the whole world." [4]

A transcended individual is guided by her own internal compass and navigates life in an autonomous manner. The definition, need, and benefit of having self-transcended, conscious individuals in the world will be discussed in further detail in a coming chapter.

The top of the axis of consciousness, which sits at the peak of the Well-being Pyramid model, represents human transcendence. However, many nonduality wisdom traditions believe in the ultimate level beyond human transcendence, which is the collective consciousness—a non-dual, unified, enlightened state. Here, you have fully immersed yourself with the Divine: your ego has dissolved.

Both Barnett's seven levels of consciousness and Maslow's hierarchy of needs speak to the evolution of human consciousness and inform the axis of consciousness of the Well-being Pyramid. All four points on the base of the pyramid (mind, body, soul, and space) will rise together along their corresponding edges of the pyramid toward the pinnacle as each dynamic evolves together with your rising level of consciousness and wisdom.

As you become wiser, your mind starts to consider far more perspectives, regulate emotions better, seek more information, utilize empathy, exercise self-awareness, and adapt. As wisdom is gained, your nervous system is better regulated and less likely to store unprocessed emotions and trauma, as the mind-body connection works optimally to recognize and move through emotions. There is deeper access to intuition and gut feelings that can be understood as body wisdom. As consciousness increases, a wise person's soul takes the lead, and one views the world through a lens of compassion and humility. More thoughtful decisions will be made. There will also be a deeper, more meaningful connection to one's space. The wise human has access to the conscious wisdom of the natural world, providing an input of profound intelligence from one's environment, both physical and non-physical.

With this understanding of the Well-being Pyramid model, let us now discuss each dynamic in greater detail, starting with the mind in Part 1. Since we are living in an extremely mind-dominated world, it makes sense that this is the first point to be described in the next chapter.

CHAPTER 1 REFLECTIONS

Note: Please choose and start a new journal that you will use to respond to reflection prompts throughout the reading of this book. A free printable journal containing all reflection prompts is available to you via the link at the beginning of the book.

Experiencing chronic, debilitating conditions led me to question many aspects of my life, including, "What does well-being mean for me now?" and "is it possible to improve my well being despite all the health setbacks?" I believe each of us is here for personal growth and evolution. It is through doing so that we gain a better well-being. It has been helpful to examine the different facets of my life and take an honest look at the areas that need improvement and those that are already strong and fulfilling.

It was also clear to me that my health and wellness and fun and recreation had reached all time lows at some point due to illness and disability. The wheel of life assessment (included in Reflection question 1 below) was at first so disappointing because some categories of my life were lacking.

However, I realized I was evaluating these categories based on my life prior to health conditions. This pushed me to really consider how I might fulfill these areas in my life despite the present reality. For example, what might fun be for me now? What might well-being in health entail? Perhaps it is to ensure I have assembled a health care team (holistic or allopathic) that makes me feel safe and assured.

Well-being lacks a universal definition, and may be best defined by your own personal decisions and commitment to your sense of safety, peace, and fulfilment.

1. How is your well-being in each of the major areas of your life? Use the attached Wheel of Life map, rate your well-being in each of the major areas of your life (career, wealth, health, family, friends, personal development, romance, fun, physical environment) on a scale of 1 to 10. [Image credit to © 2014 Whole Person Associates, Inc. Wellness Coaching for Lasting Lifestyle Change, 2nd Edition Pages 132 & 299 101 W 2nd St, Ste. 203, Duluth, MN 55802 800-247-6789, *books@www.wholeperson.com*, www.wholeperson.com]

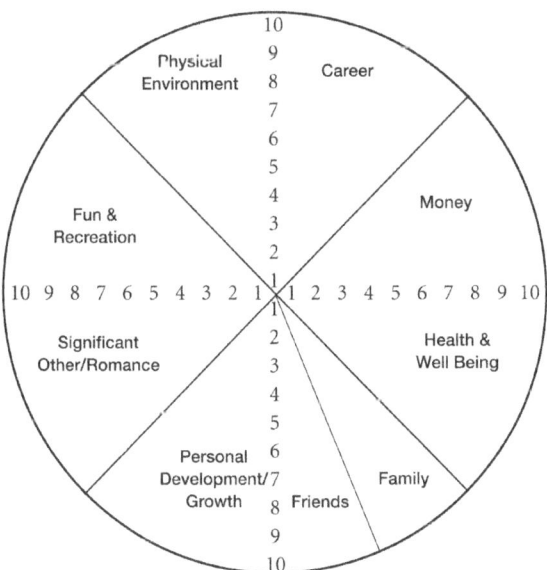

Figure 3 The Wellness Wheel of Life

2. For the areas in which your rating was less than you'd like, journal to reflect on why this may be and what may you change to improve your life satisfaction in that area? What do you want more of in your life? What do you want less of in your life?

3. What do you feel is your current level of consciousness according to Barnett's framework? What, if any, setbacks have caused you to drop to level 1, survival, mostly living in fear?

4. Are there any areas of your life in which you currently feel great dissatisfaction? Do you feel stuck? Reflect on the reasons for your dissatisfaction or stagnation.

5. Do you desire to explore or move to a higher level of consciousness? Reflect on what that looks like for you, who or what changes would you bring into your life to support that desire?

Part 1

Life hurtling by, wind of gale force.
Teetering legs threatening to topple.
Fear and uncertainty of the mystery illness pushing them to.
Test after test. Nothing to show for it—Just pain, weakness, numbness, fatigue.
Neuro visit and confirmation, "No, it's not MS."
Mind untethered and flapping like the car dealer's inflatable tube man.
Crying about exclusion from a club to which no one wants membership.
Such is the mind and its desire for certainty.

What Drives Us?

The mind is the first point on the base of the Wellness Pyramid that we will be discussing. This is because I feel it is the most easily accessible to modern humans living in a world that has been largely designed to leverage and value our mental faculties above the other dynamics of influence defined in this book—body, soul, and space. Knowledge has been power for a great many years, and intellect has reigned supreme.

Before we begin, I will provide a brief origin story of my illness-to-well-being journey. The story is pertinent here because, in one fell swoop, my sense of mental well-being was dismantled, and the reality of my health suddenly did not fit the mental image I had of myself.

DEFINING MOMENT: WHEN LIFE TOOK A PRECARIOUS TURN

For the first thirty years of my life, I considered myself healthy. I could eat what I wanted, had strength, a decent amount of flexibility, muscle tone, shiny hair, and took my perceived wellness for granted. That changed after I delivered my first child.

I was rushed to the hospital and admitted in May 2002—two and a half months after I delivered my daughter (my first)—and I was in tremendous pain, one I didn't understand. Burning, stabbing electric sensations hassled my upper back, and I could no longer walk a straight line. I was admitted to Torrance Memorial Hospital in Southern California and promptly seen by an assortment of doctors, including a neurologist. A full MRI scan of my brain and spinal cord revealed extensive inflammation in the cervical region of my spine. I would have been more terrified in this life-threatening situation if I hadn't been so exhausted.

Up until the day of hospitalization, I had been breastfeeding my new infant and feeling like I was getting the hang of being a new mother. My husband and I had purchased a condo in Redondo Beach the year before, on the Pacific Coast Highway. I loved that place. It was one of many new condos built above a parking garage and a few restaurants that were slated to open soon. At the condo level, it was beautiful, with giant potted flowering plants. I could smell the ocean air from the beach a few blocks away. I thought I'd see my daughter grow up there, take her first steps, and say her first words. I still held out hope that this thing that had happened to me, whatever it was, was a one-time fluke, and I would soon return to my healthy state.

Further tests revealed that I had lost a great deal of strength in my right leg and arm. Every point from my hip to my big toe was so weak I could barely lift my leg. I needed a cane to walk, and when I attempted to step with my right leg, my foot would swing out to the side because I couldn't raise it. My toes crumpled under when I set my right foot down.

The neurologist came so frequently to test my reflexes that I became very familiar with his tests and the points on my extremities that he would tap with his reflex hammer. I had no reflex responses in my right leg and arms. Not only had I lost strength, but I also lost other sensory abilities. I heard doctors describe it as transverse myelitis, or inflammation of the spinal cord, but there was no definitive diagnosis.

I could not sense temperature differences on my skin or in my body. My proprioception had diminished, meaning I no longer had a sense of where in space my leg was. When I sat upright with my feet touching the ground, within a minute my right foot would just slide out. I could barely feel the seat under me. I fell off more than one chair due to my wayward right leg and the lack of sensation in my hips and buttocks. I struggled with insomnia and crippling anxiety. Never in my lifetime would I have imagined myself undergoing such pain. Even the soft touch of a cotton sleeve brushing against my upper arms felt like a razor blade.

My husband brought me pictures of my newborn to keep me going while I was away from home. Looking at them caused me such anguish that I just put them away. When he could, he'd bring her to the hospital to visit. I'd attempt to hold her when he placed her in my arms, but I could only do so long enough to smell her sweet baby head.

She'd start to wiggle, and my arms would quickly lose strength. I felt her slipping away in more ways than one. All the bonding we had been doing felt undone, like we'd never be able to have that closeness again. Breastfeeding was replaced with me sitting alone on the hospital bed, attached to a breast pump, watching the milk collect in the bottle, and knowing that I was no longer producing an amazing, nutrient-rich food that would nourish my baby girl, but a poisonous, medication-laced substance that had to be extracted and discarded.

Was this to be my life now, I wondered—disabled and in constant intense physical pain, unable to be the mother, wife, sister, and daughter I had once been?

I did not know then that this journey of illness would stretch over two decades. The initial condition for which I was admitted was undiagnosed and would remain so for years. So began the rotating carousel of misdiagnoses, trial-and-error treatments and medications, and countless doctors. I had subsequent debilitating episodes of loss of almost all fine motor function in both arms. Hormonal, gut, and other issues wreaked havoc on my system. Through this experience, I struggled to make sense of what had happened to me, why it had happened, and how I could improve my situation.

The lesson I learned over time was mental fortitude and resilience. I was faced with the torment of managing my mind through all this. There were non-negotiables I had to implement just to save whatever sense of hope I had left. I decided I would not, under any circumstances, compare myself to others. I would not dwell on the way my body used to work. I would not regard myself as a victim. I would never blame another for my circumstances. Sometimes I struggled greatly with these, so it was a process.

Although it was not a conscious choice then, I fully believed this was not a permanent state, that my eventual future would be one of health and vitality. These were pivotal choices that aided my spiritual growth, even though I did not realize it then. There have been many moments of great pain, anguish, despair, fear, hopelessness, and suffering, but I choose not to make those my enduring story. Instead, they serve as checkpoints on the road to spiritual mastery. I continue that journey today.

It is only now, twenty-two years after that first hospitalization, that I have realized the greater optimism, health, aliveness, and an unwavering sense of purpose that came out of introspection, self-compassion, and the relentless pursuit of being well. Through this, I came to care very deeply about holistic well-being and what that could be for anyone, even someone who is on the illness side of the illness-wellness spectrum.

I have learned a lot about well-being through the loss of it and the gradual, deliberate uphill climb to feel and live well again. Often, it takes pain and adversity to gain wisdom about life and insight about ourselves. I've done my best to impart my learnings about well-being and alignment in this book, and my hope is that it helps you on your own wellness journey.

My life experiences demonstrated for me the importance and necessity of mental well-being. To improve our well-being in this regard, we have to learn more about the human mind.

Humans are creative, adaptive, social creatures. Our brains are complex, and with our thinking minds, we have been able to create systems and structures that have allowed us to thrive. We have overcome the hurdles of survival and meeting our basic needs to become a species that has thrived. We live in relative comfort compared to our ancient ancestors. But this has not served every human life. Too often, the wealth and "success" of the few have come at the expense of the many.

The mind, the thinking brain, has led us through an evolution from lower level "reptilian" instincts to our present state. It is debatable what exactly we have now become. Homo sapiens evolved as a new species about 300,000 years ago.[1] We evolved for millennia with basic survival being the main driver. Humans adapted, migrated, and invented tools to increase their chance of survival.[2] It is only in the last twelve thousand years or so that humans moved from hunting/gathering to an agrarian lifestyle.[3] This was the inception of modern civilization. As we developed increasingly sophisticated tools, equipment, machines, and technology, in tandem we developed more innovative brains. Through the mind you are able to perceive, think, solve problems, and identify yourself and what surrounds you.

At the base level, we have physiological needs originating from our bodies, informing our minds of thirst, hunger, the need for warmth, etc. Even the simplest of organisms respond to these needs, driven by an innate impulse to maintain homeostasis, or a balanced physiological state. With humans, needs and drives become very complex because of our higher cognitive abilities. Our minds translate physical needs into psychological drivers that motivate action.[4] It must also figure out how to get what we require for survival. .

What is the well-being of the mind? This concerns mental health, which is a very pertinent topic considering the current state of the world. However, they are not the same. Wellness refers to an overall holistic quality of being and feeling well. Mental health defines how well the mind is functioning. The Global Wellness Institute defines wellness as "an internal resource that helps us think, feel, connect, and function; it is an active process that helps us to build resilience, grow, and flourish."

What is meant by the phrase "peace of mind"? The dictionary defines this phrase as a state of mind in which the individual feels safe and secure. This means physical safety, but it also refers to psychological safety. It is with your conscious mind that you perceive your world and evaluate whether you are safe.

Assume you are able to satisfy your basic needs—food, water, and safe shelter. This is level one of Maslow's Hierarchy of Needs, defined in the previous chapter. Assume you have a community to which you belong—a family, a religious organization, or your work environment. You have connection and significance within that group. You identify with the group. This is level two of Maslow's Hierarchy. Mental well-being depends on this sense of belonging and connection, which is level three. Poor mental well-being can impact mental health.

Now suppose the group with which you identify and from which you derive significance, such as a local culture, has stipulations regarding what is and isn't acceptable for belonging to it. You may have personal beliefs or an identity that is not acceptable to that "tribe." Perhaps you are LGBTQ+, and your culture, family, or religion labels that as wrong. Or perhaps your partner is of a different race or religion, and your group rejects this union. You are then at odds with the very entity that provides you with identity and significance. This can wreck your mental well-being.

Self-esteem, level four, provides you the confidence to individuate from the group and pursue achievements of your own choosing. Here, you exercise motivation from within rather than being solely motivated by what your group has stipulated as important. If you have sufficiently satisfied level four, self-esteem, you can then begin to prioritize factors like autonomy, purpose, and growth. These fall under self-actualization, level five of Maslow's Hierarchy.

Autonomy is self-determination. It is the "liberty" and "pursuit of happiness" as stated in the United States Declaration of Independence. When your personal truth is at odds with the group that shapes your personal identity, and you have a certain level of agency to determine the course of your life, you are faced with a choice. Do you trade belonging and significance within the group for personal autonomy and self-determination? It is an exceedingly difficult decision.

You must either succumb to the edicts of the group and deny your personal happiness and identity or stand firm in your personal beliefs and risk losing the love, albeit conditional, of your group. How does a person make such a choice? It is not without some amount of fear. Fear can paralyze you, or it can act as a springboard to action. Fear may cause one person to retreat, take cover, protect themselves, or hide, but for another person, it may be a catalyst for personal growth and expansion.

There is another quintessentially human longing—purpose. The search for one's purpose is a search for meaning. Purpose drives us to strive for something more. It is an existential need to find a way to demonstrate value to oneself, a higher power, or others. Purpose is the point that guides an arrow toward a target. It can be specific to an individual or a group. A purpose can be the source of strength under horrendous conditions.

In the 2013 *Psychology Today* article written by Steve Taylor, PhD, titled The Power of Purpose, the author references *Man's Search for Meaning* written by Holocaust survivor Victor Frankl.[5] Taylor writes that Frankl observed that fellow concentration camp prisoners who maintained their purpose were the ones who were most likely to survive the atrocities. It seems that purpose is a tangible manifestation of hope, providing people with the motivation to act or to endure.

That motivation can be determined by external factors, such as the impetus to perform well at your job so that you don't lose it. Such external motivations can give people a purpose in life. Or the motivation can come from within. This is called intrinsic motivation, which is the desire to pursue something for the enjoyment or satisfaction of it. This stands in opposition to the fear and avoidance of a potential negative consequence such as being fired. Intrinsic motivation is linked with mental well-being, and it is self-determined. Intrinsic motivation can lead to personal growth.

How is growth related to well-being? Personal growth is a key factor in psychological well-being.[6] It is intrinsic growth. The highest level of Maslow's hierarchy is self-actualization. As humans we have a drive toward this peak experience—to be the best self possible. When personal growth is done with the intent to serve others, one may transcend the self. This will greatly improve mental, psychological, and emotional well-being.[7] One of the best ways to improve your own sense of well-being is to serve and help others.

The spiritual teacher and author Michael Singer says to strive for inner well-being. He says that our minds become preoccupied with wants and needs. It distracts us from the core desire in all of us for well-being. According to Singer, the mind is forever fixated on two questions, "How do I get what I want?" and "How do I avoid what I don't want?" He warns that your will (energy) may become fixated on external motivations and on how to "manipulate" life. This induces useless worry and neurosis, much like a metaphorical hamster continually running on a wheel, and thinking it is getting somewhere.[8]

Our thought processes can push us toward positive choices that improve our health and well-being. The technology and innovative tools and machines we have today were developed through the ingenuity of human minds. These innovations were achieved to solve a problem, save resources, particularly time, adapt, improve the quality of life, or because of intellectual curiosity. Humans are ever resourceful creatures and we will continue to innovate in the future.

Is there a tipping point at which any innovation can become maladaptive, and the harm it causes outweigh the benefits? Perhaps the harm is to human well-being. In the next chapter we will discuss what prevents or hinders our minds from achieving and maintaining this state of inner well-being of the mind.

CHAPTER 2 REFLECTIONS

These days, there is so much said about finding one's purpose that it can feel daunting to do so. One might believe that it must be something quite significant or considered a worthy pursuit by the external world. It is important to remember that finding one's purpose is really about understanding oneself better. What is important to you? What would you choose to do with your time even if you were not getting paid to do it? There may not be one ultimate purpose one has in life; there may be several. The discovery and connection to a purpose will help you gain insight into who you are as a person. The most important relationship one will ever have is the relationship with oneself.

1. Describe a difficult event that greatly impacted your life. How did you first react when it happened? How did you make sense of it? How did it inform the story you told yourself?

2. What was a time when you either broke away from or wanted to make a choice in your life that was not acceptable to or understood by your family, friends, or community? What was the impact on you for either making or not making that choice?

3. Define autonomy within the context of your life. How much autonomy do you have in your life? If it is not as much as you would like, what prevents it?

4. What is your purpose in life? If you have realized your purpose, reflect on steps you have taken or intend to take to move into that purpose. If you have not determined your purpose, what do you think has blocked you from determining your purpose?

5. What does personal growth mean in your life? What areas in your life will or does this growth impact?

Mind Traps

In the last chapter, we discussed what enhances the well-being of the mind. The adaptability and creativity of the human brain, which evolved from ancestral times, are some of the greatest strengths of the human mind. With that comes the desire and drive to learn, grow, and make an impact. In this chapter, we cover ways we undermine our mental well-being and sacrifice our innate capabilities.

As a kid in the late '70s and '80s, I remember times when I would think, "I am bored and I don't have anything to do." This was typically during long summer months away from school. I'd go to the kitchen to report my boredom to my mom, who would promptly send me away with a "Go find something to do." And I would. I might spend a few minutes hanging my head upside down over the edge of the sofa, imagining I was walking on the ceiling. Or I'd get on my bike and find any available friends to commiserate in the boredom. Inevitably, it led to wild creativity—building forts in my friend's backyard or inventing a new game to play. That was boredom decades ago. It created free time and space to be imaginative. With a device on hand to occupy our attention at any given moment, would a child be likely to refrain from using it and choose physical activity and face-to-face social engagement instead?

Although I appreciate the convenience the internet, email, and social media platforms have provided, I am heartbroken about the repercussions of building tools that have been purposely designed to negatively affect the mental well-being of its users. In the 2020 documentary *Social Dilemma*, Tristan Harris, a tech ethicist who had worked for Google, states that "we have moved away from a tools-based technology environment to an addiction and manipulation-based technology environment".

The PEW Research Center 2024 report states that across all five of the main social media platforms (You Tube, Tik Tok, Instagram, Snapchat and Facebook), one third of teens are on at least one of these sites almost constantly. Almost half of teens state that they are online almost constantly. Per PEW, this has risen from twenty-four percent about a decade ago.[1]

We are training whole generations of people that whenever they are bored or feeling disconnected, they can just reach for their devices and "fill" that void. Harris also stated that the platforms are digging deeper into the human brainstem to take hold of and prey upon kids' sense of self-worth and identity.

The Social Dilemma goes on to explain that the algorithms that drive these platforms have been optimized for the business platforms, where revenue is largely from advertising. Since advertisers are the true customers, the platforms are designed to maximize engagement, often at the expense of our attention and mental health. In this system, we are not the beneficiaries but the raw material. As we scroll, click, and engage, we also generate the data that trains the AI, refining its ability to capture even more of our time.

An entire book could be written on all the ways we sabotage our mental well-being. We have great reverence for the intellect, the thinking mind. Humans have made extraordinary achievements and technological advances thanks to how well we've used our minds. Yet in the United States, 22.8 percent of adults–almost 57.8 million Americans–experience mental illness. 5.5 percent have severe mental illness.[2] Something is terribly wrong with the way many of us are using (or not using) our minds.

According to the yogi expert, founder of the *Isha Foundation*, and modern-day mystic Sadhguru, the "intellect is like a knife. You use a knife to cut things open. This is the nature of the intellect. Whatever you give it, it will dissect."[3]

However, when used incorrectly, our intellect can also wound us—it's like a knife afterall. Long before modern science, Eastern scholars studied the mind by deeply exploring themselves. It was understood that the mind constantly chatters, demanding something to ponder, mull over, to pick apart and analyze.

According to Buddhist tradition, the mind is like a restless monkey. Constant mental chatter signifies the uncontrolled monkey mind. Mindfulness and other forms of meditation have always sought to subdue this chatter.[4] It was known thousands of years ago that we are not our minds. The search for mental health and well-being can start with becoming observers of our own minds. Ekhart Tolle in his book *The Power of Now* writes, "The single most vital step in your journey toward enlightenment is this: learn to disidentify from your mind." Tolle's reference to the mind includes its thoughts and emotions.

There are innumerable ways your mental wellness can be derailed. Devastating external events like war, abuse, loss, and poverty can traumatize our minds, and upend our most basic survival needs—shelter, food, and safety. The mental impact may be experienced for a lifetime, or even across generations.

However, it doesn't take extreme events to disrupt mental well-being. Even in our everyday mundane lives, we must contend with the voices in our heads. Think of those moments when your thoughts are racing, and you are preoccupied with rumination. Do you catch yourself and bring your mind back to the present and to a state of mental calm?

Unaware of their origin and impact, we may fully identify with these random, incessant thoughts which may be negative and critical. To quote Dan Harris, the author of *Meditation for Fidgety Skeptics*, "When you are unaware of this ceaseless talkfest, it can control and deceive you. The ego's terrible suggestions often come to the party dressed up as common sense."[5] One's ego may play the role of a harsh taskmaster, an abuser, or may overly inflate one's sense of self through arrogance, pride, or selfishness. Ultimately, this could result in a distorted self image or an egregious lack of compassion.

A healthy ego may begin as a necessary aspect of being human. It is through your ego that you establish an individual identity in the world. The development of the ego has been integrated into the growth and development of a baby. An infant's ego begins to form within the first few months, coinciding with the infant's differentiation from its mother and driven by its interaction with its physical environment. The ego serves the vital purpose of helping us create our individual identities. The problem arises when you become more identified with the ego identity than with your internal self (more in Chapter 10 on the authentic self). Over-identification with the ego leaves you more prone to negative mind states such as worry.

Why do we worry? Worry, fear, and anxiety—three "siblings of doom"—seem to go hand in hand to undermine well-being. However, there is an advantage to these negative feedback loops our minds can conjure up.[6] They have kept us alive. Those with a more finely tuned radar for potential danger are the ones more likely to recognize and avoid it.

I have always found it odd how much we seem to love doomsday storylines. Dystopian movies have had considerable box office success. Books and movies like *The Hunger Games, Maze Runner, Divergent, Minority Report,* and *The Matrix* paint a bleak and often harrowing future for humankind. Why do we watch them?

Per a Psychology Today article titled, "*Why Does Watching Dystopian Shows Feel So Good?*" watching these movies helps us to practice emotional regulation in a safe environment. They allow us to escape a current reality that we find distressing into a fictional, imagined one. These stories often present an underlying message of hope and humanity's ability to persevere through exceedingly difficult circumstances.[7]

In real life, repeatedly worrying about potential future events pulls you out of the present. This is not ideal for a state of well-being. As the spiritual teacher Ekhart Tolle writes in *The Power of Now*, "Realize deeply that the present moment is all you have. Make *now* the primary focus of your life." Tolle describes the past and future as "delusions of time". Regrets can significantly decrease your mental well-being as energy is stolen from the present to ruminate on something that has already happened which we wish had a different outcome. We all understand the logic of this, yet succumb to its pull.

The poet Khalil Gibran wrote, "Yesterday is but today's memory, and tomorrow is today's dream." Worrying or dwelling on events that have already passed or that may never happen tethers the mind to unhelpful thoughts. That focus is better directed toward positive and productive areas.

Sometimes even focus that is beneficial proves to be challenging to achieve in today's world. The phrase "attention economy" rings true in a world saturated with social media. Everyone is vying for your attention, your likes, comments, and often, your money. We seem to be getting more distracted without even getting to choose what distracts us.[8]

The lure of the incessant social media feed is potent. It's affecting all of us, but the most alarming is the impact to young, developing brains. We have yet to ascertain the far-reaching impacts of the loss of focus on young minds.

Another thought pattern that can become unhealthy is comparison. People have compared themselves to others since the beginning of time. Comparison serves the evolutionary purpose of pushing us to do better. When our self-esteem is intertwined with the ongoing results of these comparisons, our sense of self-worth can plummet if we feel we don't measure up.

In psychology, social comparison theory explains that people evaluate their own abilities and achievements against those of others. We compare upward with people of higher level of status, achievement, or abilities. We also compare downward with others we see as not as capable as we assess ourselves to be. Either way, social comparison is a source of stress.[10]

FOMO, or the fear of missing out, happens because of comparison.[11] There is a deep-seated need in us to belong to a group. Its roots lie in the tribal communities from which we evolved. Belonging to a group ensured a greater chance of survival for the individual. FOMO is another mind condition that creates mental stress and saps our authentic energy. Energy is dissipated outward, and we attach our well-being to external factors. We seek belonging because humans tend to feel less stressed when bonded with others.

Social media ratchets up the potential for FOMO. If you are a person with social anxiety who is attempting to feel a sense of belonging and to quell feelings of loneliness through online means, you are more prone to feel this sense of disconnect as you view other people's posts where they seem to be living an enviable, full, and social life. Once again you are outsourcing your sense of self and well-being to external entities. This inevitably leads to greater unhappiness or even depression.

You are also at a higher risk for FOMO if you already have low self-esteem. This can have a negative impact on your physical health as well, causing headaches, body pain, increased heart rate, and stomach pain.[12] It's time to take control of your sense of self. Identify and align with your inner values. Focus on what strengthens your self-worth and makes you feel good. What brings you joy? What pulls you down? You must remember that the solution to the problem is not external, but within you. We must teach our young people to attune inward to affirm self-worth. How to do this is addressed in Chapter 5 on nourishment of the mind.

There are other unproductive ways we undermine our mental well-being, notably blame. Shame and vulnerability researcher Brene Brown, says "blame is about the discharging of discomfort and pain. It has an inverse relationship with accountability."[13] Whether in a workplace or within your family, blaming someone for an outcome that did not have the result you wanted is at best counterproductive. At worst, it is wounding to the person or people on the receiving end.

Why do we resort to blame? The one inflicting blame on others is shifting their regret, disappointment, guilt, or anger to an external target to escape those emotions themselves. There is a self-esteem component in this; by placing the focus on someone else, the blamer attempts to preserve their own sense of worth. Yet, this avoidance of personal responsibility and emotional discomfort ultimately erodes well-being.

This same pattern applies to self-blame. Instead of projecting emotions outward, a person may turn them inward, harshly judging themselves for not meeting their own perfectionist standards. True self-acceptance involves understanding and accepting that we are all imperfect human beings who deserve grace for our mistakes or shortcomings. One can accept responsibility for their contribution to an undesired outcome without resorting to self-blame.

Mistakes and negative outcomes are inevitable, and how we process them, depending on our mindset, significantly affects our well-being. Stanford psychologist Carol Dweck developed the concepts of growth and fixed mindset. A person with a growth mindset believes that they have the capacity to learn and grow, despite their limitations. A person with a fixed mindset believes that the level of their intelligence and capabilities is static. They tend to believe an outcome is one of two possible states—success or failure.[14]

The growth mindset reframes mistakes and failures as opportunities to learn, grow, and improve. A growth minded person accepts accountability for the outcome, and sees it as a learning opportunity. They channel their energy towards examining an outcome and developing an improvement, instead of funneling blame for failure to a person.

Individuals with a fixed mindset limit their opportunities with "all-or-nothing" binary thinking. This is a cognitive distortion. It negates any other possibilities and can produce negative emotions and mental states. An August 2022 article in Psych Central titled "*What Is All-or-Nothing Thinking and Why It's Important to Manage It*" states that this binary thinking can lead to anxiety, depression, PTSD, and personality disorders.[15]

To be human is to be perfectly imperfect. You live a human experience, which is your "school" to learn from and grow. When you dwell in creativity, expansion, and curiosity, you have the opportunity to build positive outcomes, solve problems, and nurture other people. It seems so simple, yet our thinking mind is both our greatest asset and biggest obstacle.

While intelligence has propelled human progress, our deep reverence for it has often come at the expense of our well-being. The relentless drive to expand our intellectual and technological capabilities has led us to remarkable advancements—but at what cost? In the next chapter, we will explore this drive in greater depth, particularly how it has given rise to artificial intelligence. As we push the boundaries of human ingenuity, we must also consider how these advancements may shape, challenge, and impact our well-being.

CHAPTER 3 REFLECTIONS

"Words are energy and they cast spells, that's why it's called spelling. Change the way you speak about yourself, and you can change your life." — Bruce Lee

Your relationship with yourself is the foundation upon which rests your quality of life, health, and well-being. Your self-talk—which includes your tone, words, and intentions—is a reflection of this relationship. Be a compassionate and loving friend to yourself. You have the choice and ability to ensure the self-talk voice encourages and soothes rather than criticizes and increases stress. Strive to separate yourself from the voice of negative self-talk. It is not you. You are the awareness that is observing that voice.

1. What is your experience with being in silence with your thoughts? For what duration can you do this?

2. Journal prompt: What are your recurring negative thoughts that cause worry, anxiety, or fear? If you are unsure about them, journal on this prompt every day for a week to uncover negative patterns and their triggers. Then next to each negative thought write the present tense positive opposite of that thought. Example: I have a fear that I will not have enough money to live / I am so grateful to have an abundance of wealth

3. What topics of information do you click on in social media? What is in your feed of your most used

applications? Who do you follow? How does the content make you feel about yourself and your life?

4. Journal prompt: How do you handle getting a negative outcome (failure) from something you tried? What messages do you tell yourself? Do you cast blame or self-blame?

The "Optimized" Mind

At twenty-two, while working as a counselor at a children's summer camp, Nolan Arbaugh unknowingly dove into waist-deep water head first and hit an object in the water. This resulted in a devastating spinal cord injury which paralyzed him from the shoulders down. In January of 2024, Neuralink, a company co-founded by Elon Musk, successfully implanted a chip in Nolan's brain, which enabled him to control a computer or smartphone with his mind. The chip was surgically implanted and threads from the chip were connected directly to his brain.[1] Receiving this technology has been a gift for Nolan, who is now able to navigate a screen, peruse the internet, and play music.

Per Nolan's own words, he was excited to be the first human to have received the device and hopes this will help other paralyzed individuals. Neuralink is now seeking individuals with quadriplegia for the first clinical trial.[2] The optimization of the mind through brain-computer interface (BCI) technology certainly provides hope to improve the well-being of individuals who can no longer navigate the world through their bodies alone.

Since the beginning of time, humans have developed ways to make their lives easier, be more lucrative, and become more powerful. We are what we are today because our ancient ancestors devised tools to facilitate the quest for food and shelter. From crude stone hand tools to the irrigation systems in ancient cultures like that of Mesopotamia, we have invented, built, and optimized ingenious ways to acquire what we need and more. The thought has been that better innovation will increase our well-being.

Fast forward to the present day, where we have connectivity between most of the global human population via the internet, wireless communication, and phones with computers that fit into our pockets. Our economic systems, which have become extraordinarily complex, reflect our needs and desires for accumulating resources. We have had every opportunity to create for the betterment of all global citizens and with a reverence for our planet and its gifts; yet as a species, we find ourselves still warring, exploiting, and taking more than we need. It seems we view life as a zero-sum game—if someone acquires something of material value, there is that much less available to everyone else. Therefore, one person's gain then becomes another person's loss.

Collectively, humans keep taking lives, biodiversity, and minerals without much regard for what or who gets hurt or exploited. We act as if growth and productivity, economic wealth, power, and control represent the ultimate pinnacle of achievement.

We ceaselessly fight, kill, and create endless trauma for ourselves and others. As long as humans continue to act in ways that serve to undermine rather than enhance our well-being, the technology that is implemented will reflect these negative choices, often creating long-lasting trauma in the process.

We are on the precipice of a new age in human technology that appears to be advancing faster than we can control—an age of artificial intelligence. Currently, AI is a tool to extend human capabilities. A tool is not inherently good or bad. Recall Sadhuguru's analogy of the hand holding a knife. The knife is neither good nor bad, but how conscious is the hand that wields that knife? That is what determines what will be done with it. There are many warnings floating around about the potential danger in creating a human-like mind that is purely rational, that is, without a conscience.[3] It is likely that AI intelligence will quickly surpass human intelligence. The Center for AI Safety warns of creating AI systems we cannot control.

How does AI fit into the mind dynamic of the Well-being Pyramid? We have software we use to manage the complexity of our current systems. In that sense, we are enhancing our minds' capabilities and reducing the time, effort, and inherent human error that would result from doing these activities with our minds alone. GPS systems are ubiquitous in our world. It's hard for me to remember how I navigated spatial directions without GPS. I will admit I am directionally challenged, so these navigation apps on my phone are vital to me.

In a sense, I have outsourced those tasks to a "brain" outside my own. There are only a few phone numbers I have memorized, whereas prior to phones that store these numbers, I had memorized dozens. Is my mental well-being enhanced by these applications? Well, I have less stress knowing I will not get lost and that I have hundreds of phone numbers on hand if they are needed. On the other hand, my life was fine prior to having these capabilities. With the technology has come an overall push to complete tasks with more efficiency and with minimal or no errors. Technology has informed a new expectation. Perhaps we feel compelled to adopt the latest innovations or risk falling behind in a world moving at breakneck speed toward an uncertain future. In that regard, we are not using technology as much as technology is using us.

We developed the computer originally to help us with calculations, to compute. Then they became machines of productivity, designed to enhance our lives and make our work more efficient, accurate, and quicker. That drive has pushed us to develop better, smaller, faster technology. As we optimized for efficiency, our machines got smaller and more powerful.

AI seems to be a natural progression of this human desire to think faster, more accurately, and at a scale that the human mind cannot achieve on its own. There is also the consideration that we humans have created for ourselves some catastrophic issues in the way of climate change, pollution, food scarcity, chronic disease, etc. AI offers the potential vehicle for solving our massive global problems as well as enhancing human life on a personal level. We seem positioned to outsource our well-being to artificial intelligence, with the belief that the human mind alone cannot solve the issues we created.

Currently, the technology sector seems determined to incorporate AI into every facet of our lives, so that we become more productive and efficient. There are millions of beneficial applications of AI in progress: using health data to proactively screen for cancer and other diseases, tools to aid people with disabilities and mental health, to help solve our climate crisis by studying climate data and using predictive analytics to understand the potential future damage, and to address world hunger by optimizing crop development and distribution.[4] These are just a sampling of the myriad promising uses of AI that will potentially increase overall human well-being.

There are numerous positive benefits for the human mind that can come out of AI development. Both the accessibility and personalization of learning positions artificial intelligence as an optimal solution for providing flexible, personalized learning for each person at a fraction of the cost of the educational institutions we have had for centuries.

Emad Mostque in a discussion with Peter Diamandis on Diamadis's podcast *Moonshots* described a project underway via the XPrize for learning in which they are teaching literacy and numeracy to groups of children in Malawi Africa for one hour a day within 13 months using adaptive learning. Their system doesn't require the internet and involves the use of tablets incorporated with AI. He stated that soon this will be completely customized to the child and work with different learning styles and learning disabilities. Mostque believes that knowledge and learning are a basic human right and these learning models will be open source.[5]

I have been following the nonprofit company Khan Academy for many years and appreciate the free grade-specific personalized learning they offer to students, as well as life skills, and tools they make available for teachers.[6] Khan Academy has launched Khanmigo, an AI tutor. It also acts as an AI-powered teacher's assistant, curriculum developer, lesson planner, among other things.[7]

Per a June 2024 Forbes article, the U.S is grappling with an enormous mental health crisis with demand for services far exceeding the number of psychotherapists.[8] AI therapy is poised to fill that void thanks to its ability to deliver a range of mental health services including cognitive behavior therapy and personalized strategies. AI chatbots can offer non judgemental and informed therapy at lower cost than that offered by traditional therapists, making it more widely accessible. Companies like Woebot Health, which offers a Cognitive Behavioral Therapy (CBT) based chat, are looking to make inroads into the therapy space.[9] There are dozens of platforms like Woebot, such as Ollie Health, which proposes an AI wellness coach, presents visual mental health data metrics and is targeting corporate mental wellness.[10] Youper also uses CBT techniques to provide mental health support via chat.[11] It will be interesting to see if AI therapists can actually replace human therapists and produce successful results.

AI can be used predictably using patient records and tracking behavior to proactively flag signs of mental health issues such as depression or anxiety using predictive analysis. This can inform the mental health practitioner of the patient's vulnerability to some of these issues. Patient's written communications such as text, email, or speech can be used to ascertain the patient's emotional state. Faces can be scanned to assess emotional state.[12] Of course the handling of personal information must be executed with HIPAA and privacy in mind. Intention is key, so who will be privy to this data and for what purpose they will use it are the pressing questions for AI application in mental health.

How might AI tackle human companionship? Loneliness from lack of meaningful connection has been determined to be a significant health risk and a mental health and well-being issue. The previous U.S. Surgeon General Dr. Vivek Murthy observed the level of disconnection and loneliness as he traveled around the United States. He writes in his book, *Together: The Healing Power of Human Connection in a Sometimes Lonely World*, that "loneliness is the subjective feeling that you are lacking the social connections you need." He describes three types of loneliness: intimate (wanting a partner/close friend), relational (friendships), and collective (community of others with shared purpose/interests).[13]

Can AI fill the gap and provide companionship for those who crave it? Perhaps it can advise, assist, and encourage humans to take action to find companionship. As our world has become increasingly digital, with more daily hours spent online (the average is six and a half hours worldwide), we become increasingly isolated and lonely.[14]

Companies like Replika offer AI companions as a coach, partner, or mentor. I am left to wonder what it means for well-being if a person's closest friend is an AI bot instead of a living, breathing human with which to co-regulate one's nervous system? On the positive side, Replika tracks its user's mood and provides deeper emotional support. But, perhaps AI companionship can lead to further isolation of a person from other human beings. Also, these AI companions cannot address collective loneliness in which community still entails human community.

Aside from these, there were glaring issues that caused the company to close operations in the United States. The Italian Data Protection Agency banned Replika's use of user data in February of 2023. Many users had been interacting with their bots as romantic partners. Replika's decision to remove the ability to have erotic conversations with their users was met with considerable pushback. The case of Replika points to the responsibility such AI companies have when making AI that engages with humans on an emotional level.[15]

In terms of our mental habits of doom scrolling on our phones, dissociation via Netflix, and the attention-hijacking capabilities of social media, AI is playing an increasingly active role. AI is generating social media posts, delivering targeted content to our feeds, and suggesting streaming content catered to your demonstrated interests. AI will only become even more adept at serving up content that is more effective at capturing your attention.

All of this development has made it even more imperative for people to have a deep, holistic knowledge of themselves and what it means to be a human being. The optimization of the human mind via technology is beneficial to well-being in specific use cases but can be significantly detrimental to well-being in others, as illustrated by the examples described above.

This is where the Well-being Pyramid can be an essential framework for your alignment and well-being so that you are not just looking for these answers outside yourself. Through the WP, you take full accountability and ownership of your well-being and your personal identity as a human in this ever-changing world. You determine and acquire the resources to help you on your journey to becoming a fully aligned human. If a particular technology truly optimizes your quality of life and well-being, then you may decide its incorporation into your life is beneficial. Some of these choices are individual ones. You may decide not to engage with AI applications, for example. Some of these choices are collective, and we must consider how they impact all of us as a whole.

It is crucial that we take a holistic view of any technology being developed and optimized. The questions must be asked, and investigations must be conducted. Who is this technology benefiting, and how? Is human well-being central to that benefit?

Thus far, as a collective, humans continue to be prone to wars and violence and to baser instincts and inclinations, such as greed and the thirst for power. We continue to value competition over cooperation. As long as we are "othering" people and assigning their well-being a lesser value than our own, we are in danger of destroying ourselves and potentially our planet.

How do humans evolve to be the fair, compassionate, and cooperative beings we have the capability to be? This hopeful version of evolution is one I believe we are moving toward, albeit very slowly, and despite the tumultuous political, social, and economic climate of this year—2025. I remain optimistic that we are gaining momentum and that the overarching desire of humans will be to help one another and act with compassion. Let us work toward a future in which we share our resources and care for the planet through regenerative and nondestructive methods.

Can we develop our technology in line with the most ideal of human qualities such as empathy, kindness, honesty, caring, generosity? Also are we going to take a long term view in the development of AI with regard to who we would like to be—a peaceful, prosperous humanity, as opposed to segmented, distrustful countries separately vying to gain a foothold and dominance in the AI space for their own agendas? Well, the way we do business would have to change, including the incentives for making change happen, levels of transparency, open source sharing, and quality of support for those organizations for whom human well-being is the central mission.

Conscious capitalism is a starting point. It includes the principles of higher purpose, all stakeholders included in the whole "business ecosystem", conscious leadership and culture.[16] Cynics may disagree and declare the impossibility for our entire global system, as interdependent as it is, to shift to a conscious economy. Investors want to see profits. But, one cannot underestimate the power of conscious individuals working together to create change. This has proven to be true in countless examples, such as in boycotting companies with undesirable ethics or pushing for positive environmental impact. How well a company treats its employees can be indicative of conscious capitalism. Costco's millions in charitable donations, commitment to its climate action plan, its animal welfare policy, and its current status as the largest organic grocer are some of the factors that demonstrate conscious capitalism.

Sustainability has been incorporated into the economy through the efforts of individuals and activists raising awareness, speaking out, demanding better. Conscious individuals prioritizing efforts like the conservation of natural resources, protection of the environment, elimination of harmful chemicals from our products, and support for future generations have done and continue to do the beneficial work of shifting the public's sentiments and rallying them for change.

The well-being question remains front and center in the development and optimization of technology like AI being touted as the answer to many of the issues we currently face.

It is one we must all address. AI provides some powerful opportunities to better our lives. It can also undermine quality of life if we don't exercise the forethought and examine the motivations behind large-scale AI development.

AI looms as an enigmatic and powerful force that is capable of doing good or evil with an aloof indifference, not unlike Dr. Manhattan in the *Watchmen* DC Comics comic book series. In the *Watchmen*, the character Jon Osterman becomes Dr. Manhattan, the quantum being of unlimited power.[17] To me, this character is less a superhero, and more a metaphor for AI–emotionless, dispassionate, and purely intellectual. In the story, the American government uses him as a weapon in a warring, antagonistic world. Giving something that lacks consciousness and empathy the power to make decisions and take actions that impact our collective well-being seems like folly on a grand scale. We are not there yet with AI technological development, but is that around the corner?

So, our species is at a crossroads. Do we continue developing advanced technology without sufficient wisdom and forethought, while polluting and overconsuming earth's resources, and killing one another? Or do we make a concerted effort to develop ourselves—our own minds—to optimize for empathy, compassion, love, and a deep reverence for all life? The latter will guide our technological developments and the optimization of the human mind toward collaborative, united societies.

The road to that outcome depends on each human doing the inner work to resolve trauma, restore well-being, and foster compassion for themselves and for others. It depends on the human collective working diligently together to clean up the messes humankind has created to date. The next chapter delves into how might each of us do the inner work, foster mental well-being, and heal.

CHAPTER 4 REFLECTIONS

Time feels accelerated as we rush toward an unknown future. Most humans want their future to be an improvement on the present. They want their children and children's children to have an even higher quality of life than they have had. When I look at the evolutionary history of humans, there is ample evidence that millions of years later, we have far improved in areas like technology, medicine, education, and food distribution. But are we better humans than we were in the past? I suppose it's a matter of perspective, but this question leads to "Who do we want to be?"

How we develop and use AI will be pivotal in achieving or falling short of any envisioned future. It is only after defining who we want humanity to be as a future species that we can establish the parameters of AI design and use. So, instead of designing technology for the world we have now, the vision should be for the world we want to manifest. That encompasses the broadest radius of global humanity and all the concentric circles included within—country, region, community, family, and self. What characteristics will the future you embody, and how will those personal traits ripple outward to impact the larger societal spheres?

1. The Values Card Sort

   (https://www.motivationalinterviewing.org/sites/
   default/files/valuescardsort_0.pdf) is a motivational
   interviewing exercise developed by Dr. W.R. Miller.
   It is used for individuals to determine the values
   most important to them. Complete the exercise for
   yourself and journal your top five values within the
   list of values most important to you.Then do the same
   exercise to determine the top five values that you feel
   should be incorporated in AI design

2. Reflect on your thoughts and feelings about the
   increased use and integration of artificial intelligence.
   What are the boundaries in your own life that you
   feel must be implemented to protect your mental
   well-being as AI becomes more complex and more
   integrated in making decisions about how all of us live?

3. What do you envision as a future utopia with humans
   and AI? What AI technologies do you use in your
   personal and/or work life?

4. How do you feel about using AI technology to address
   mental well-being? What are the benefits of using an
   ever-accessible chatbot that has been trained in therapy
   modalities and emotional responsiveness? How does
   your answer change when you consider interacting
   with a bot that is not truly empathetic?

Nourishment of the Mind

In my youth, I played an Indian stringed instrument called the sitar. As I became more adept at both fingering the notes with my left hand and striking the strings using a "mizrab" or pick on my right index finger, playing the notes became second nature. I was a dedicated student, as I adored the instrument and the music it could produce. As I grew more skilled, the "ragas," or arrangements, increased in complexity. I reached a point when I could play many ragas from memory. Not only that, but I learned the advanced skill of "pulling a note," or using the fingers of my left hand to slide the string along the fretboard to bend it to another note. The result was a more complex, rich, expressive sound.

When I played, everything else fell away—except my music. I was in a state of flow. Flow is a very positive mental state we attain when there is an optimal balance of one's skills with the challenge level of the task. Flow, first named and defined by psychologist Mihaly Csikszentmihalyi, can be induced in any area of activity that meets the criteria. One can be in flow while running a marathon, painting, solving puzzles, or gardening, for example. Flow state is ideal for mental well-being. Here the brain is getting flooded with feel-good performance neurochemicals like norepinephrine, dopamine, endorphins, serotonin, and anandamide. Activity in the prefrontal cortex is temporarily lowered. So your self-consciousness or tendency to self-reflect, is offline. Your mind is "in the zone", focused, and engaged.[1]

The neuroscientist Dr. Caroline Leaf explains that though the mind and brain are connected to each other, they are two unique entities. The mind shapes the brain and changes it. According to Dr. Leaf, the mind operates as an energy system. When we think and experience emotions, it generates electrical signals, which are triggered by sensory inputs from the external world and processed by the brain.[2]

Dr. Leaf writes about using the mind well and avoiding attempts to multitask. Essentially, when we are in flow state, we are focused on one task, our mind's energy is concentrated, and we are engaging the mind in a positive manner. This is heightened energy management. As a result, flow state produces a deep intrinsic motivation and desire, and serves to reduce anxiety and stress. We can choose to engage our minds in ways that are deeply nourishing.

We know through our minds that we are alive. We tend to recognize and equate the mind with ourselves, our identity.

Common idioms involving the mind, like "out of your mind," "peace of mind," and "change your mind," demonstrate how we identify our thoughts, behavior, and well-being with our minds. Without realizing we have agency over our mental well-being, we may fully identify with our emotions and thoughts since they come from our thinking minds. We may feel at the mercy of whatever feeling comes into our awareness. Our minds may also attribute the source of that feeling to some object or event outside of ourselves.

The WP has been designed to visually separate the mind from You as pure awareness or the Observer. From a Buddhist perspective, grief is a process, not merely one emotion. Tenku Ruff, a Soto Zen Buddhist priest, states "it [grief] is a process—a continuum of emotions that unfolds at its own pace."[3] So even in grief, you can be the awareness or watcher of these heavy emotions. This means that you feel the emotions and acknowledge their presence, until the emotions pass. The grief cycle may repeat many, many times through the course of healing, but nothing is permanent. The suffering of sorrow shall pass too. Even our brains are not in a fixed physical state, as studies in neuroplasticity have shown us.

Neuroplasticity is the brain's ability to change its structure and function. It can create new neurons (neurogenesis), change and even create neural pathways. Humans can care for and improve their brains through the mind. The opposite is also true—a troubled, depressed mind damages the brain, decreases its size in some areas, and can increase the size of the amygdala—the part of the brain that processes anger, fear, and sadness.

Selective serotonin re-uptake inhibitors (SSRIs) are most commonly used to treat depression. Given that depression is now a global health issue on the rise, there is a push to find treatments that help alleviate depression more quickly than the two to four weeks required of SSRIs. Also, it is desirable to find solutions that do not introduce lasting side effects. Ketamine and psychedelics like psilocybin, MDMA, and LSD may provide more rapid relief and improvement. Some individuals with treatment-resistant depression find SSRIs to be ineffectual. Psychedelics have been found to increase the neuroplasticity of the brain in certain cases.[4]

Use of these drugs come with a lot of caveats as psychedelics administered without the professional expertise, control, and study, i.e., recreational usage, can have grave negative consequences. I mention these alternatives as an example of the need for continued innovation and study in the area of mental health to find the most optimal and efficient way to restore mental well-being. It's exciting to observe how these and other novel therapies may be further developed and integrated into psychiatry/psychotherapy in the future.

Through our minds, we determine our reality. If the brain is the hardware with which we create our realities, the mind is the software that utilizes this hardware; yet it is this software that can structurally alter the hardware. All our sense organs are receivers collecting input. We process what we see, hear, feel, taste, and smell with our brains. So, what is received by the senses and how it is interpreted, based on recognition from a past experience or newly constructed from pieces of other past experiences, enables the mind to create its reality. Our mind categorizes what it sees and through "ad hoc construction". It has the ability to create new categories and assign value to what is being perceived.

What can we do to care for our minds? American author and motivational speaker Jim Rohn said, "Stand guard at the door of your mind." He meant that the perception of our reality starts with thought. What you let into your mind or consume becomes your reality. If you want to live an inspiring and dynamic life, minimize or eliminate the negative, fear-inducing thoughts that threaten to render you hopeless. This includes what you read and watch, who you have around you, and the institutions and people with whom you align and spend time.

This one act of filtering out negative mental inputs helps to unburden the mind from having to process and "digest" the negativity of the external world. It makes sense that the more negativity you experience, the more likely you are to perceive the world as a place of fear, hatred, and violence. Your mind will seek to confirm that perception with every new input and experience.

In addition to the above, select and absorb uplifting, positive, supportive information. What is your mind ingesting daily? Do you stream twenty-four-hour news channels? Do you immediately grab your phone and start scrolling social media once you wake up? As much as TikTok may provide true and useful information and learning, there is an enormous amount of misinformation as well. Also, the use of platforms like TikTok comes with all the potential trappings of addiction to a screen, toxic comparison, and the sensory overload of having to process a great deal of "data" very quickly with little or no time for the space of reflection, contemplation, and creativity.

I consider myself a lifelong learner. I have been alive and participated in the rise of the internet. When I first perused websites in the early days of internet adoption by the public, it was a magical way to freely learn just about anything. But the internet, like any other human-made dispenser of information, is a double-edged sword. More than ever, we must consciously select what we feed our minds. Like the old Native American adage of the two opposing wolves within each of us, the one you choose to feed grows strong within you.

Your mind creates your ego, personality, and identity. This is the "I" or "me" with which you refer to yourself. Observe your mind. Name that part of you from which a negative emotion arises. For example, "Ah, that is my ego creating a feeling of envy when I see my neighbor's new car." Start noticing, get curious, pay attention to the inputs you give your mind, and to the thoughts, feeling states, and emotions that result. As you strengthen this skill, you will more easily be able to distinguish what causes negative, fearful, or angry emotions to arise. Notice what you do, if anything, with those negative emotions.

Engage regularly in a "world view check in", during which you objectively determine what the world represents to you. Is the world a fearful or unfair place? Do you feel it is marching toward an inevitable dystopian reality? Is the world magical and ripe with synchronicities and opportunities? Determine what makes you feel more positive about the world and yourself. Be the watcher of your mind and the cultivator of your positive mind state.

Practices for strengthening the mind and alleviating mental suffering have existed for centuries. For Eastern philosophies like Buddhism and Hinduism, mindfulness and meditation have been mainstream practices that have been steadily gaining followers throughout the world. More than ever, we need such tools to nourish the mind.

Mindfulness is a state of being in any given moment, and meditation is one way to practice it. Mindfulness is now a part of mainstream Western vernacular but has its roots in Buddhism. It is the seventh of eight paths or facets of life as delineated in Buddhist philosophy.[5] Mindfulness is an ability that every person possesses—to be fully aware and tuned in to the present moment. This practice frees you from dwelling in the regrets of a past that no longer exists or the worries of a future that has not and may not ever happen. Mindfulness frees your mind from the exhausting cycle of negative thoughts. Mindfulness helps reduce stress and improve focus. This mind-nourishing practice trains you to become a curious observer of others, the world, and your own mind.

In meditation, you are blocking out external stimuli, quieting the mind, and striving for non-thinking. Transcendental meditation (TM) is part of a larger category of mantra meditation that involves the repetition of a short sound.[6] One must be taught by a certified teacher who will instruct you on the sound you are to use in your mediation. The sound is assigned only to you and you do not share it with others.

In TM, the goal is to transcend our superficial thoughts, by a simple and natural process. As intrusive thoughts arise, you gently turn your attention back to the mantra. Over time you can go deeper into the stillness within. There are hundreds of research studies that prove the effectiveness of TM to address stress, anxiety, depression, as well as many cardiovascular and other physical and mental issues. A few studies are cited in the Chapter End Notes. [7, 8, 9]

As we care for ourselves in our daily habits like brushing our teeth, showering, and drinking water, so should we regularly nourish our minds. Our minds help form our thoughts, and our thoughts become the reality we experience. Quality thoughts support a healthy, resilient mind, which in turn impacts your overall well-being.

In the next chapter, we will begin discussion of the body in Part 2 of *The Aligned Human*. I will address the body as the second point on the Well-being Pyramid. We will take a look at various paradigms we have used to understand the role and function of the body, the body as interconnected systems, and how to nourish the body.

CHAPTER 5 REFLECTIONS

My view of the world as a threatening or nurturing place was based on the experiences that I had mentally stored, even without realizing it. It was colored by my family's level of fear and uncertainty as immigrants in a foreign country striving to survive. That had been embedded in my psyche from a young age, and I did not even realize it. I carried within me the fear of my maternal grandmother suddenly widowed with eight young children, my sixteen year-old father included. I carried that fear within me as a silent unacknowledged threat to my survival even though their experiences were not my own. It would manifest throughout my childhood as a terror of the dark or the fearful thoughts that my parents would suddenly die.

When I first became gravely ill, disabled, and hospitalized, I was forced to face that old fear of survival for the first time. Some years into my illness journey I noticed that those fears were gone. I had been through something unfathomable, debilitating, and scary. Yet, I was still here. My world view had shifted. The world was no longer such a daunting place. Even while facing the uncertainty of an unknown illness, I could now see the world as full of possibilities. Those possibilities included my ability to heal and overcome my health obstacles.

1. Journal about a time when you were in flow state. What were you doing and why was this a state of flow? Reflect on the feelings you remember while engaged in flow

2. Finish the sentence: The world is a place of… Then write five examples of why you view the world this way

3. What are your beliefs about your mind's ability to change, adapt, and grow? What does growth mean to you?

4. What do you do to alleviate stress and anxiety? Write three examples and categorize each as either an exercise that reduces stress or just provides distraction

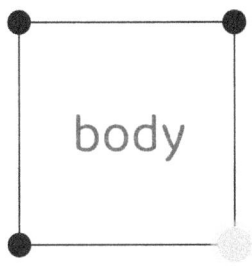

Part 2

Central line placed in jugular vein.
Pain as it goes in and now makes its home in the body.
Plasmapheresis.
Machine and body are one circuit and blood is the electricity.
Is the body a machine?
Seems like it right now.
Can plasma exchange remove the auto-antibodies of uncertainty,
fear, and grief?
Maybe then, they won't seize control.
Laying still as blood is filtered for the offenders.
Autoimmunity is the body's confusion between self and non-self.
Time to re-acquaint and make friends with my body.

CHAPTER 6

Body Metaphors

I laid very still on the gurney and waited silently for someone to take me to Imaging for yet another MRI during yet another hospitalization. I had been wheeled into a hallway and left there for some reason. There was nothing to do but be with my thoughts and try not to catastrophize possibilities in my mind. I was too scared to even slightly shift because I had widespread loss of sensation in my torso and was petrified that one slight movement would cause me to fall off the gurney. I couldn't sense where on the gurney table my body lay, so I stayed very still—yet impatient. Had I been able to, I'd have sat up, jumped off the gurney and gone to find someone to hurry the process along.

The tears streamed down the sides of my face, making their way toward my ears. I felt discarded, forgotten, like I was an object instead of a person. I might as well have been the gurney in the hallway. There was zero regard for my fears or my well-being. It seemed that nobody had the time or empathy to help. When I look back at that time and my thought that my body had betrayed me, I realize I had no real understanding of my body. I viewed it as a collection of parts–muscle, bone, flesh, organs. I understood that my nerves permeated my entire body, but there was no "fix" offered for that part of the body.

The MRIs showed visible inflammation in a section of my spine, but no one could answer for me why or how that had occurred. There was a suspicion of an autoimmune condition, but at the time bloodwork did not confirm anything. Had I known all I now know, I would have understood that my body is a complex series of interconnected systems, and autoimmune conditions are not contained within a system. I needed to address the root cause of inflammation, nourish the body, and allow it the time, space, and compassion to heal itself. This event was the inception of my lessons and learnings on how to heal the body.

The body is the second point on the base of the Wellness Pyramid, and is a vital component of overall well-being. The amount of respect we have for our bodies is reflected in our behaviors that either harm or nurture our physical form. The metaphors we use to conceptualize the human body become significant to the type and quality of care we choose to provide and the resulting level of well-being that will be experienced.

Container

Do we see our physical form as a container, with each of us living as contained systems—bodies with mass and volume separate from each other, all living beings, and the environment? Are we three dimensional containers filled with mind, soul, emotions etc. completely separate from other life forms? I have heard the body referred to as a "meat sack", as if all that is held within the confines of our skin "container" is flesh and bone. To use this metaphor is to reduce the beauty of the complex, dynamic, interconnected systems of the body to an amorphous blob. This metaphor does little to garner respect and admiration for the body that tirelessly works to support us.

Machine

The body is a mechanical machine, like a car. If we can't repair a body part, we strive to replace it. The mind is often given high status as the master with the body acting only in service to the mind. This mechanistic approach has largely influenced the framework of Western Medicine in which specific parts are relegated to corresponding medical specialities.

Traditional or western medicine separated the body from the mind and compartmentalized organs or organ systems into parts. We have specialized doctors for each major organ system, whether it is a cardiologist, neurologist, gastrointestinal specialist, dermatologist, or any of more than a hundred specialties in medicine. In addition, we have specialized doctors for aspects of the mind/brain such as psychiatrists and neurologists. This metaphor grossly simplifies and overlooks the many dynamic processes, such as electrical and chemical processes, that occur outside of our conscious control and navigate across both mind and body.

There are interconnected "parts" that traverse the whole body, such as fascia and cannot be isolated and treated separately.

Fascia is the connective tissue network throughout the body. A region of fascia restriction can be treated to release tightness, but this is not an individual part of the body. Here, the body as a machine metaphor does not hold up.

Battleground

The human body is a battleground in an ongoing war between good (immune cells) and evil (invaders, bacteria, viruses, cancer). These metaphors have endured in support of the current disease model of western medicine. We need to kill cancer cells or suppress the immune system (render it ineffective). The aggressive and militaristic conceptualization of how disease is handled completely negates all the beneficial and necessary functions of the body, as well as its innate ability to heal.

As a result, we may destroy cancer cells but kill healthy cells in the process. We may shut down immune function that is dysregulated, as in the case with autoimmune conditions. However, immunosuppressants increase the risk or likelihood of certain diseases, and this goes against the very reason the immune system exists in the first place - to fight infections.

A warlike mindset focuses on "killing the bad guys" at all costs—inexclusive of the protective healing mechanisms intrinsic to our bodies. We are often left with a weakened body that is less able to engage its natural healing processes. I am not maligning these approaches to stave off or lessen the devastating effects of these illnesses in the short term. While it can help prolong someone's life, I simply ask "At what cost?"

and "Can we find a better approach?" In order to do so, this line of inquiry should not be closed off because we choose to stick to the paradigm of doing battle with disease.

Energy

What about the metaphor of the body as energy? Signals are constantly transmitted throughout the body through electrical signals. Our body's electrical system utilizes nerve cells (neurons) and synapses to transmit electrical signals throughout the body. The body converts the chemical energy stored in food into Adenosine Triphosphate (ATP), energy that fuels each of the cells. There are metabolic pathways that create and utilize energy to allow the body to function.

As an example, the body absorbs energy from the sun and utilizes that energy to produce essential nutrients like vitamin D, 90 percent of which is obtained through this means. It is then metabolized in the liver and activated in the kidneys. Vitamin D affects calcium levels in the blood, so your bone health depends on it. Vitamin D is absorbed to a smaller extent (10 percent) from food and influences how well calcium is absorbed by the gut.

A deficiency of vitamin D not only adversely affects bone health, it impacts the body's ability to successfully fight infections, and impacts the body's energy by reducing fatigue through support of the cells' mitochondria. It is the mitochondria that provides a body with the energy it needs to function.[1]

The metaphor of the body as energy, or energy systems works exceptionally well to demonstrate the interconnection of humans with the natural world and nature's role in vitamin D production. Swallowing a Vitamin D supplement daily is one way to meet our needs for that essential nutrient, especially when one lives in a climate with very little sunlight. But one must consider our deep and beneficial connection to our natural environment, and how nature provides for us. These are the energetic characteristics of our existence.

Humans gain so many benefits from moderate sun exposure such as improved sleep quality, energy levels, immune function and mood. Humans evolved with and through the planet's natural environments. This is but one example of the body as energy interacting with energy outside of it.

Another example of the body as energy is earthing, which is a practice of grounding oneself to the earth. This can be as simple as placing bare feet on the ground. Humans used to walk barefoot or in leather-soled shoes, and sleep on the ground. Most of us do not do this today. These practices kept us connected to the Earth's healing properties and reduced the body's cellular inflammation, which is now a known precursor to chronic and aging issues such as autoimmune diseases, cardiovascular disease, cancers, and depression. The Earthing Institute is an excellent resource for research studies proving the benefits of earthing.[2]

Metaphors are mechanisms by which we make sense of complex ideas and systems. The body as energy works well within the Wellness Pyramid framework. Energy and the body are discussed in greater detail in a subsequent chapter in which ancient Eastern healing modalities as well as energy healing practices are described. The following chapter describes complex systems to further support the systems biology at work within our bodies.

CHAPTER 6 REFLECTIONS

My body, my enemy. There were many years during my illness trajectory during which I tried to not feel my body. This unconscious disconnect came as a result of great discomfort, fear, and hopelessness that I did not know how to get myself out of constant pain. This disassociation was a survival mechanism during a period when I felt my body was failing me and I did not know where to go for solutions. Life didn't stop and I had to carry on despite these circumstances. I was living the opposite of an embodied life. At that time, my body felt like a heavy, cumbersome mechanical suit I had no choice but to bear.

When I finally reached a point where I realized that whatever I was doing (or not doing) was hampering my health and longevity, I had to face my relationship with my body. This was a first step to reclaiming it. I made myself pay closer attention to physical and feeling sensations. Where in the body did a sensation occur and what thoughts and emotions were present at the time? It was a slow, steady process of coming back to a state of love and care for my body, instead of constantly rejecting and feeling betrayed by it. These were my first steps to reconnect mind and body. It started with recognizing that after illness, I regarded my body as a burden, something separate from me. We are not the mind or the body, but alignment with the mind and body we have been given is required for health and well-being.

1. What is your metaphor for your body? How well does that metaphor align with events in your life that have impacted your body, such as illness, injury, or disability?

2. How well do you know your body? How do you describe your body? How well does your body support you?

3. Pay close attention to your body's messages about energy. What causes you to feel low in energy? What replenishes your energy best?

Holistic Body as Interconnected Systems

It is important to speak about the paradigms we use to treat illness in the body and to optimize the body for true well-being. The western medical model of disease, diagnosis, drug profile, and treatment, with its compartmentalized specialties, does little to incorporate the interconnectivity of multiple systems, holistically address the human being, and bring a person back to a full state of health. This model is not adequate for reversing complex chronic conditions that may ravage our bodies over time. We need a better paradigm that more accurately helps us conceptualize the body and its functions.

When you are struggling with poor health or debilitated by illness, it is not likely you will feel a sense of well-being. I know from my own health journey that when you are experiencing symptoms that persist or worsen over time, you often feel betrayed by your body—believing that it is working against your well-being. This is certainly true with autoimmune conditions, in which your immune system is attacking its own healthy tissue, mistaking it for an external threat.

As a college student, I took a few systems theory classes, which included systems analysis and design. A set of components in relationship with each other can be studied as a system. The relationship between components, input and output of each entity within the system, and the flow of information are all factors to consider in systems analysis. When I took a class called biocontrol systems with the goal of applying systems analysis to biological systems, I realized the layers within the human biological system that present extremely complex sets of relationships.

Incidentally, artificial intelligence can provide an exceptional way to model and analyze complex human biological processes, taking into account the myriad of inputs both internal (from the body) and external (from the environment.) For example human immune function has a key role in autoimmune diseases, but making sense of the complexity requires understanding processes that affect our physiology on a multitude of levels. Per a November 13, 2024 *MIT Technology Review* article, "the immune system alone involves interactions between millions of cells, proteins, and signaling pathways, each influencing the other in real time."[1]

These are interrelated, interdependent entities. When looking at something from a systems view point, you are considering the function, structure, and role of each component, and the interrelationship between the components. Each component is dynamic so each can affect any number of the other components.

A simple system, such as a recipe for cake, is made up of components within a fixed, known system. The components may interact, but in a known and predictable way. One follows the steps outlined in the recipe, adds each measured ingredient, mixes, and bakes. The inputs are the ingredients, the output is the finished cake. A more complicated system, such as the game of Monopoly, is considered a "bounded interactive system." The rules are fixed, and each player interacts within the boundaries of the rule set. Any one of the players might win at the end of the game.

What about a complex system? A complex system has many parts, with each part dynamically interacting with any number of the other parts. The most optimal way to understand a complex system is to look at it holistically, because there are so many interacting processes that are occurring. Patterns or traits become apparent that describe the system as a whole. A complex system is "dynamic, unbounded, incomplete, contradictory and constantly changing." One cannot definitively predict the outcome.[2]

The financial market is composed of many systems that influence each other, such as the stock, bond, and other securities markets. Rising interest rates may cause bond rates and consumer spending to decrease. The stock market valuations may decrease. The Federal Reserve, the governing body that sets interest rates, may raise rates to stave inflation, thereby increasing the price of goods, and decreasing consumer spending. If this rate increase is too aggressive, those entities participating in the market could get worried about a recession and that can impact their spending, thus causing volatility in the market. It is impossible to accurately predict an outcome in a complex system with great success. The behaviors of any of the entities participating in the system can impact one or more of the other entities. The best thing an investor can do is to understand market trends and relationships.

Just like the financial market, the human body is a complex system, composed of many other complex systems. Systems biology, an interdisciplinary area of study, is "a holistic approach to deciphering the complexity of biological systems that starts from the understanding that the networks that form the whole of living organisms are more than the sum of their parts."[3]

There are holistic modalities that incorporate the complexity of the human body by treating the whole person. Ancient cultures in China and India developed holistic medicine, and those traditions and learnings are still practiced today. In recent times, the Western medical world is starting to wake up to holistic possibilities, and this has given rise to fields like epigenetics.

Epigenetics, per the CDC is "how behaviors and environment can cause changes that affect the way your genes work." These modifiable lifestyle factors will not change the actual DNA but can switch gene expression on or off. We now have a growing area of lifestyle medicine which focuses on those positive epigenetic changes that lead to true disease reversal.

Also, every individual is unique. A therapy or medication that works well for one person can wreak havoc on another. This realization has led to the rise of precision or personalized medicine, which addresses the reality that there is no one-size-fits-all solution since each human is different, with unique genetics, environment, lifestyle, and cultural drivers.

Other fields of medicine such as, integrative medicine, which integrates complementary and alternative therapies with traditional medicine, functional medicine, which is dedicated to finding and resolving the root cause of the ailment rather than just treating symptoms, and naturopathic medicine, which combines traditional medicine and modern science for providing alternatives to the traditional western medical approach, seeks to treat the whole person.

My personal experience with naturopathic doctors has been very beneficial, as these physicians have a broad array of knowledge from natural solutions to traditional western medicine; they can also recommend either or any combination of solutions as it best serves your health needs.

It is so encouraging to see that our understanding and concept of the human biological system is evolving toward a more holistic paradigm—one that can incorporate the complexity of living organisms. Perhaps the key to successful treatment and prevention of complex chronic diseases within western medicine lies in changing the model to one that incorporates a systems approach and better reflects the complexity and interconnectedness of the body.

The body is an interconnected array of systems and processes that have been beautifully designed to support health and well-being. We have been gifted with a natural world that is designed to support our body's health and well-being, but still suffer because we have forgotten that interrelationship, and subsequently decimate the planet. We will discuss the natural environment in the later chapters about space and our relationship to it.

As a collective, we are witnessing a transformation in what it means to have well-being and health in today's modern world. The old paradigms are shifting, and both ancient traditions and new innovations are providing more integrated solutions. We have novel threats to our physical health because of stressors like climate degradation, pollutants, toxins, sedentary lifestyles and occupations. This changing landscape and the growing demand for more effective methods to address health concerns world-wide urges us to scrutinize and reassess what it means to be thriving, healthy humans. A holistic approach to health and well-being means that you are addressing your mind, body, and spirit. This is why the Well-being Pyramid encompasses all those facets of well-being, as well as space. The relationship between well-being and space will be discussed in later chapters. In the following chapter we will dive into how to nourish the body.

CHAPTER 7 REFLECTIONS

Finding my way to better health has been a process of understanding the interconnectedness of the multitude of processes continually occurring in the body. This became particularly evident in the relationships between my adrenal, thyroid, and sex hormones and the resulting imbalances I encountered, starting with the experience of high, prolonged stress and my adrenal gland's overproduction of cortisol. The high levels of cortisol led to disruption of my thyroid hormone production and hypothyroidism. All of these hormone disruptions coincided with perimenopause and sex hormone imbalance. This led to an interference of the delicate progesterone/estrogen hormone balance, and I experienced it as anxiety, pain, and sleep disruption.

So what had been a beautiful, dynamic system of hormones in balance became a disorderly cacophony of hormones out of sync. It took some years to reduce the stress and balance my hormones. Of course, this is a very simplistic explanation of the hormone systems of the body. Exogenous factors like toxins and chemicals greatly impact as well. It is essential to get the full picture of what is going on with your body. Simply singling out one symptom such as anxiety, and medicating for that would have been insufficient to truly address the issues.

1. What are some examples in your own life that demonstrated to you the interconnectedness of systems in your body? How did these impact your well-being?

2. What has been your experience with holistic medicine? What holistic therapies have you found that have helped improve your health? What are you curious to try?

Nourishment of the Body

Sometimes it can feel challenging to stay on top of taking care of the health and well-being of your body. In the modern world, our lifestyles and social systems are integrated with fast, processed, chemical-rich, and/or inflammatory ingredients, such as seed oils widely used in restaurants or emulsifiers, artificial dyes, and preservatives.

Alternatively, there are many factors to consider and incorporate into your regular routine. Eating nutrient-rich meals and snacks, moving and exercising daily, getting adequate sleep and rest, and consistently engaging in self-care activities you find beneficial will positively influence your well-being and help keep your body well. Let's take a look at each of these factors.

Food

Food. It's a loaded word. To each person it brings up different feelings. There may be joy and a sense of belonging and community. There may be desire, craving. Perhaps one feels fear, insecurity. Depending on your life circumstances, and your past experiences, food conjures a multitude of thoughts and emotions.

Food as "fuel for the body" is integral to the metaphor of our bodies as machines or vehicles. It implies that the human body is a machine with working parts. If a part malfunctions, one attends to the faulty part. But the body is so much more, and these reductive analogies do not do justice. Food is much more than an energy source for our body. It is information and medicine, and the quality of the food you eat matters.

A calorie was first discovered in the early 1800s in relation to the efficiency of steam engines. Engines convert heat into work that drives the machines. It was in the late 1800s that calories were defined to measure the energy in food that when consumed could be utilized by the body. By the late 1800s, the U.S. government adopted the calorie as an efficient measure of nutrition for the masses, originally for schools, prisons, and the military.[1]

Calorie measurements have been effective but overly simplified, and ignores other more significant measures of nutrition such as the quantification of macro nutrients (types of fats, carbs, and proteins), micronutrients (vitamins, minerals), and phytonutrients (naturally-occurring nutrients in plants that are a powerful defense for health).

Fast forward to today, we are bombarded with food choices and diet plans. The average person must sift through a deluge of information to ascertain, often by trial and error, the most optimal food choices for their health and well-being. We are tempted at every turn with food-like packaged items engineered to hijack our taste buds. We easily become addicted to unnecessary substances like sugar and the fat-sugar combination that are manufactured to provide an immediate dopamine hit.

In these instances, we tend to eat with our taste buds only, paying no regard to sensations within—how the food is chewed and swallowed, and the sensations that arise as it travels down the esophagus, moves through the stomach, continues to digest, and is finally eliminated. Often, we are distracted while we eat, relegating our dining experience to the level of a mindless activity while watching TV, working, or driving.

Eating foods that have a low nutritional quality may make us full for a while, but induces more hunger because the body is not receiving the nutrients it needs. As a fast food nation, the U.S. may very well be paradoxically malnourished. The steady proliferation of fast food chains to other countries has made this a global issue. The food is designed to hijack your taste buds, break down quickly in the mouth, and overwhelm your senses.

Fast food is most often nutrient-poor and rich in calories. It can contain high amounts of fats, sugars, simple carbohydrates, and unhealthy fats. This has implications on blood sugar and insulin levels, and fast food does not often provide lasting satiety. One may be left feeling hungry soon after eating a fast-food meal. But it's quick and cheap. It has historically been priced low enough to be easily accessible to people of lower socio-economic means, as well as adolescents. Prices have risen in recent years, yet the fast food industry is poised for growth. A Fast Food Global Forecast Report of 2025 states that this market will reach $1.25 trillion by 2033.[2]

How does an individual choose food that truly fortifies and supports the body? As a start, we must strive to reconnect to our food. Regardless of lineage, cultural roots, or ethnicity, we are here today because of an ancestral relationship to food. For much of human history, people ate sustainably, relying on unprocessed whole foods. However, in the last few centuries, a mere blip on the timeline of humanity, food production has undergone a radical transformation, especially in the Green Revolution of the 1960s.

The Green Revolution of the 1960s was a response to the prevalence of global famine, and indeed it was successful. But choices made then in terms of fertilizers and pesticides used, resulting in water pollution, soil degradation, malnutrition and the chronic health conditions we are grappling with today are indicative of the damaging effects of optimizing yield at any cost.[3]

Where do we go from here? Many are stating that a new green revolution—focused on sustainable agriculture—is underway. This movement seeks to reverse the damage caused by industrial farming by promoting regenerative practices that restore soil health, reduce chemical dependence, and protect biodiversity.[4]

At the heart of this transformation is the consumer–you. Every choice we make at the grocery store, every meal we prepare, and every ingredient we prioritize sends a message about the kind of food system we want to support. If we demand nutrient-rich, ethically produced, and environmentally responsible food, producers will be compelled to meet that demand. In this sense, consumers are not just passive participants in this revolution; they are its driving force. Our collective choices have the power to shift food production from an industry built on efficiency and profit at any cost to one that values sustainability, biodiversity, and human health.

This shift is not only about food; it is about well-being as a whole. The Well-being Pyramid emphasizes nourishment of the body as one of its four key pillars. Proper nourishment involves eating nutrient-rich, and biodiverse food, and having a loving personal relationship with food.

My past relationship with food was unhealthy. I was an emotional eater, using food to feel better. I know firsthand how difficult it is to break these addictions. Eight years ago, I had a wake-up call when I finally slowed down my life and noticed I had become obese. I started to pay attention to my body—how tired I felt, how I'd feel sleepy right after a meal, how I didn't feel like I had much energy throughout the day. But I was addicted. Left to my own will power I knew I'd struggle through weight loss.

I found a medically developed program that did the thinking for me. I followed it without wavering. This program provided food for two of three meals and snacks. It was a ketogenic diet, higher in good fats, extremely low carb, and optimized for protein, but with severe calorie restriction. During the first weight loss phase, one puts their body into ketosis. The diet is so low carb that the body will utilize your fat stores for energy.

The diet was a success and I lost forty-five pounds in five months without losing any lean muscle mass—thanks in part to my regular strength training. I do not recommend this diet, but mention it as an approach that worked for me. I was concerned about the lack of quantity and diversity of phytonutrients incorporated into the regime. Also, shifting out of this diet into normal healthy eating was psychologically difficult because severely restricting my eating for months had conditioned my mind to accept this deficit of calories as normal.

However, I did learn a few valuable things from the experience. One, it is possible to decrease the desire for sugar and fat. When I reintroduced berries into my diet, the natural sugar in the fruit tasted amazing because my taste buds were not skewed to expect high sugar hits. Two, losing the excess weight gave me more energy during the day and eliminated the desire for daytime sleep. Three, I needed additional external support to succeed in my weight loss goals.

Changing habits is a difficult process because your mind and body have become accustomed to certain inputs. Often an external support or "push" is required to overcome this hurdle. I experienced some negative results of eating dairy and sugar-loaded foods due to an unbalanced gut microbiome (dysbiosis) and other food sensitivities that developed later in life, some years after the completion of my keto diet regime.

The burning gut pain and uncomfortable esophageal reflux truly motivated me to find a way to feel better. Western medicine has some "plug-the-hole" solutions for these symptoms. My doctor was ever willing to recommend over the counter antacids or prescribe a proton pump inhibitor (PPI) to reduce my stomach acid, both of which would over time ruin my gut microbiome, destroy my electrolyte balance, and perhaps put me at greater risk for infections. These remedies are acceptable in moderation and for a short time period as a stop-gap solution. The more I learned about functional medicine, the greater my resolve became to find and address the root cause of my condition, which could have been cellular inflammation, intestinal permeability, or food sensitivities—issues that medications may exacerbate.

Food sensitivities involve the activation of the immune system through interaction with a particular food. Food sensitivities are different from food intolerances, which are a functional response within the digestive process, e.g., diarrhea, bloating or gas. Of course, one may experience similar symptoms with both conditions. For example, Celiac is an immune-mediated disease that can develop at any point in your life. With Celiac, gluten is life-threatening and must be permanently eliminated.

Allergies are the third type of food-related issue. Allergies, which can be deadly, also mediate the immune system. Both allergies and sensitivities can be determined through testing. When it comes to allergies, intolerances, and sensitivities, eating habits must be changed to improve your quality of life. Thus, you may be forced to reconsider what you will choose to consume, thus the negative push toward change.

At the lowest point in the journey to heal and rebalance my gut, I was unable to eat many healthy foods such as dairy, soy, spinach, and eggs. Eating a moderate amount would result in terrible gut burning and pain, which would lead to an uptick in my chronic neuropathic pain. I really missed eating those healthy foods. The experience of gut pain was so undesirable and painful that there was no mental wavering if I wanted to reverse my gut issues.

Processed foods were out of the question. I dealt with debilitating symptoms of both Small Intestinal Bacterial Overgrowth (SIBO) and Irritable Bowel Syndrome (IBS). The negative experiences forced diet changes as I had to adopt an elimination diet, work to heal the gut over time, and slowly reintroduce whole foods. Gluten and dairy remain absent from my diet, but I have resolved these gut issues.

Successful habit change can be implemented through positive external support from someone knowledgeable about behavioral change, such as a health coach. I recommend a coach well-versed in holistic health, such as a functional medicine coach, who will consider the lifestyle implications of the habit change. Humans are complex. There are many factors that can impact how well someone implements habit change. Knowing their cultural traditions, social circles, familial support, and environments provides a more complete picture for the health coach.

Food, personal care, and household products very often include additives, preservatives, dyes, or toxins that harm the body. When you start reading labels and becoming familiar with these additives, you will see that they are everywhere. According to the World Health Organization (WHO), there are three main categories of food additives: flavoring chemicals (derived from natural sources or chemically synthesized to imitate natural flavors or fragrances), enzyme additives (extracted from natural plant, animal, or microorganism) used to induce biochemical reactions, and other additives used as preservatives, to add color, or to sweeten food products.[5]

There is an international organization called the Joint FAO/WHO Expert Committee on Food Additives (JECFA) that in participation with the WHO and the Food and Agriculture Organization of the United Nations (FAO) assess the risk of these additives and establish standards of use.

However, according to the Environmental Working Group (EWG), the food and chemical companies in the United States have been able to circumvent the Food and Drug Administration (FDA) review and approval process through a loophole that allows them to self-determine the safety of what they produce.[6] This legal loophole allows chemicals to be classified as "generally recognized as safe" or GRAS.[7] As of the writing of this book, the Secretary of Health and Human Services RFK, Jr. is currently pushing for the closure of this loophole. The EWG lists twelve additives in food that should be avoided. These include nitrates and nitrites in cured meats, potassium bromate in flour, BHA, BHT, titanium dioxide, PFAS, and artificial colors and sweeteners, among others.[8]

Loving and caring for your body involves becoming knowledgeable about hidden ingredients in the food you eat, and replacing them with restorative and replenishing ingredients. There is a deep wisdom in your body that, when tapped into, can guide you toward health and well-being. The body is not merely a "meat sac" or shell that houses our beings. It is a sacred conduit to inner knowledge and wisdom. Every cell of the body has conscious intelligence. These concepts are discussed further in the coming chapters on the Mind-Body, Spirit-Body, and Space-Body connections of the Wellness Pyramid that represents one's full holistic embodiment in the current earthly life.

For anyone struggling to improve your relationship with food, start by noticing. Keep a food journal. Be honest about what, when, and how much you eat. How your body feels after types of food. Tune into and capture the messages from the body about what is nourishing and what is depleting. Be cognizant about how your food was made or the ingredients you use to cook your food.

Eat mindfully and without distraction. Get a realistic view of your relationship to your food. There is a ton of information about the benefits of particular foods. Start educating yourself on them. Do not be confused over which diets you should adopt. If you desire additional support on an optimal diet for you, a functional or integrative nutritionist can be very helpful. Functional nutritionists regard food as medicine, and are knowledgeable about how different foods help the body. They take a holistic approach to nutritional needs, considering your lifestyle, environment, and other factors that influence your food consumption.

There are a number of useful apps that will assist in researching the ingredients in the food, personal, and household products you purchase by giving you the ability to scan barcodes. Some of those are EWG's Healthy Living, Yuka, Think Dirty, BobbyApproved, and OnSkin for cosmetics.

Movement

Human bodies are designed to move. It's what we have been doing for millennia. Sitting for work is a recent phenomenon. Currently, about eighty percent of our jobs require sitting for extended periods of time. This sedentary work and the lack of adequate movement poses health risks. Cardiovascular disease and insulin resistance are factors that can derail our health, as is stroke, high blood pressure, anxiety, and diabetes.[9]

Clearly, we are meant to move and move often. But, how does movement nourish the body? Exercise energizes the body, strengthens muscles, increases endurance, and improves sleep.

It is unfortunate that for the majority, much of our workday includes sitting. Any changes you can make to break up the sedentary stretches of time will benefit your health.

Standing desks, sitting on an exercise ball while doing desk work, setting a timer as a reminder to rise, stretch, and move for five minutes every thirty minutes are some of the creative ways people incorporate movement in their day. In Dan Buettner's book, *The Blue Zones Solution,* he writes of areas in the world that contain the highest numbers of centenarians.[10]

Whether in the Nicoya Peninsula of Costa Rica, California's Loma Linda, Ikaria in Greece, Okinawa in Japan, or Sardinia in Italy, all the centenarians have a lifestyle which keeps them very mobile in daily living. Buettner states that the blue zone residents maintain low-intensity physical exertion throughout their day, as a natural part of daily living. This may include gardening or simply walking from place to place.

Be cognizant of and realistic about the type, intensity, and duration of movement that could be beneficial to you. These factors are very likely to change as you get older, and with additional health issues. Exercise that was beneficial to you in your twenties may not be as beneficial in your mid-forties. For example, forcing your body into a rigorous circuit training regime while wearing a knee brace due to the nagging knee pain that the same strenuous exercise produced will not be wholly beneficial to your body.

That was me five years ago. I did get stronger muscles and increased some muscle mass. However, I realized that this high impact rigor was producing negative results along with the positive ones. The "no pain, no gain" motto must be put into the context of your unique body. I later opted for a gentler, low impact form of movement that included stretching/yoga as well as HIIT (high intensity interval training) workouts on an elliptical machine to eliminate high impact on my knees.

It's important to note that your musculoskeletal alignment is very significant, and attention must be paid to this as you go about selecting and trying various forms of exercise. Knee pain may be transferred from weaker ankles and feet, misaligned hips, tilted pelvis, or shortened and contracted muscles.

If you are regularly exercising while having significant misalignment or weakness in a particular area, there is a greater opportunity to experience the knock-on effects in that or another area. There is a plethora of free content on this topic that you can sift through. There are professionals such as chiropractors and physical therapists who can give one-on-one support and advice for your needs. Pay close attention to signals in your body and distinguish between the good pain that results from working your muscles harder to increase strength, and the bad pain of an injury such as a sprained ankle.

Be creative with your movement choices. Do what appeals to you. The most important thing is that you move!

Rest

While sleep is not the only means to rest the body, it is vital for the repair of our bodies. According to sleep experts, at least seven hours of good quality, restful sleep is required for adults. Young children and teens require more.[11] Slowing down and honoring the cues from your body to rest is at the core of showing kindness to yourself.

The hustle culture that has permeated our work and personal lives encourages pushing through any pain, discomfort, and fatigue under the guise of productivity. This mindset often requires one to override their body's request for rest. Many of us require one, two, or four cups of coffee to inject an artificial and temporary burst of central nervous system activity.

The key word is temporary. However, equating caffeine with energy is problematic. It does temporarily help with focus. And depending on the quality it can be a source of antioxidants. But the amount of daily coffee and the ideal time to drink it varies from person to person depending on how quickly a person metabolizes the caffeine. The point is that when your body needs rest and cries out for it, you must indeed rest.

Sleep is important to brain function. It impacts most of the functions and organs in the body, including the brain, heart, metabolism, and immune system. These nightly repairs and restoration are essential for our health and well-being. Major areas of the brain are directly impacted during sleep.

The hypothalamus in the brain contains nerve cells that manage light exposure from the eyes and one's sleep/wake cycle or circadian rhythm. The brain stem produces the neurochemical, gamma-aminobutyric acid (GABA), which reduces arousal and activity in areas of the brain. It also sends signals to relax muscles and reduce movement necessary for Rapid Eye Movement (REM) sleep.

During this deep level of sleep, the thalamus sends signals to the cerebral cortex that we experience as dreams, and the amygdala (which helps us process emotions) becomes very active. The brain's pineal gland produces melatonin, the hormone that promotes sleep.[12]

Relaxation during wakeful hours is essential as an antidote for stress. And it feels great! Sinking into a warm bubble bath at the end of a long day can melt away the stress, giving your mind and body a much-needed reprieve. There are a multitude of benefits to relaxation, including a more normalized blood pressure, controlled blood sugar, reduced muscle tension, and improved sleep and mood.[13] Relaxation is a skill like any other. We are fortunate there are many proven modalities for relaxation through movement (Tai chi, Qi Gong, yoga), stilling the mind (meditation, mindfulness), and body work (massage, acupuncture).

Humans are social, so it's no surprise touch is an important component of well-being. Not only physically touching the body as in massage, but energy work as well. Reiki and the "laying on of hands" are alternative practices widely used for healing purposes. Energy medicine, once largely considered pseudoscience, has been garnering more mainstream interest and support.

It has its roots in ancient traditions and mystical teachings. Traditional Chinese Medicine (TCM) views a person as an energetic being with a life force called chi or qi. The ancient Vedic system of medicine called Ayurveda, which originates from India is also based on energy systems within the body. Ayurvedic science states that these energies must stay balanced for optimal health.

Both TCM and Ayurvedic remedies have helped me support my health. Most recently, I turned to Ayurveda after trying and failing to address my sinus congestion that was triggered by allergies to environmental elements such as pollen, grasses, and dust. I had been trying a variety of antihistamine sprays and pills, which were not solving the problem and, in the case of the sprays, tended to taste terrible as they dripped post-nasally down my throat. I was miserable!

Ayurveda offered an oil blend called nasya. I found it incredibly effective at clearing my nasal passages without the rebound congestion that happens if you use a nasal decongestant too often. I am in awe that these natural solutions which have been in practice for thousands of years, not only address the issue but also soothe the body. The oil helps relax my tense neck and shoulders, manage allergy symptoms, and improve my sleep.

TCM herbs were a great benefit to me at a time when I was experiencing debilitating gut pain that would keep me up at night. TCM massage and acupuncture helped me alleviate physical pain that was both neuropathic and musculoskeletal.

Energy systems are discussed in more depth in a subsequent chapter on Body-Spirit.

My direct experience with both TCM and Ayurveda is that each strives to bring and maintain balance of energy in the body. In each discipline, health is directly tied to nature through a distinct five element system. TCM incorporates wood, fire, metal, earth, and water. Ayurveda includes air, fire, water, earth, and ether. There is no one-to-one correlation between a TCM element and an Ayurveda element, not unlike how we have distinctly different languages each with the overarching and universal purpose of communication. Both ancient systems are beneficial to help energetically balance the body and optimize for a state of healing. I have experienced both systems of healing at different times and have gotten great benefit through the herbal remedies, acupuncture, massage, and dietary recommendations. We are energetic beings with soul energy. These healing modalities are more subtle in their influence, but over time I have found they are very beneficial on the path to true healing, and not just symptom management.

In the upcoming Part 3 of the *Aligned Human* we will discuss the soul as the third dynamic point on the Well-being Pyramid.

CHAPTER 8 REFLECTIONS

1. What is your relationship to food? What are your habits around food, e.g., frequency, macrobiotic breakdown (fats, proteins, carbohydrates), emotional attachment, activities during eating? Some fitness and food tracking apps you can download and try free are Chronometer and MyFitnessPal

2. How do you prioritize sleep? Where does quality sleep fall in your list of self-care priorities? How often do you reduce your quality sleep hours to do something else? In those times, what takes precedence over your sleep? If you are sleep-deprived, what would be the experience of prioritizing sleep for one week? How are energy and mood impacted?

3. How much movement do you get during your average day? What do you enjoy most in movement/exercise?

spirit

Part 3

Burning. stabbing, aching, slicing.
So many types of pain.
Days are filled with single moments.
Relinquishing the futile exercise of visiting the past or future.
Rationing pain meds for the most important times. Such as now,
as I sit cross-legged on the floor next to the baby blanket on which
my little girl crawls.
One hour of thirty percent less pain.
She crawls toward me, fingers splayed like little starfish.
As I lean toward her, she stops, looks up, and presses her lips to
mine.
This is why I continue. This is why I persevere.
I see the beauty and magic of who we are and why we prevail
despite the hurdles.
Love sees us through the hardest of times. Love carries my spirit
forward.

Belief Systems, Spirit, Soul

At 13, I visited the 800-year old Dharmasthala Temple located in the state of Karnataka in India. I had been there before as a child, but this time felt different. I was noticing more about the temple atmosphere and activities around me. I was seeking something higher and greater, although I wasn't aware then. I thought of it at the time as God. The "God" of Hinduism is represented by many different gods. But at the core, Hinduism holds a belief of one single God source–Brahman. So there I stood, bare feet on ancient stone, breathing in the camphor used to light the diyas (oil lamps) for worship and the sweet fragrant jasmine intertwined in my hair.

I tried hard to feel a sense of connection to this holy place and to the divine. I listened to the mantras being chanted in a rhythmic, pulsing way. I watched the male priests performing the puja rituals. I observed them move into a temple mantap to perform an intricate offering to the exquisitely-adorned deity statue inside, and then move out and through the crowd of gathered worshippers chanting "leave way" over and over as they left. As part of the ritual, the priests had bathed and were not to be touched by any worshipper so that the priest could remain "purified" for God.

Being there as a young teen, I struggled to feel closer to divinity. Nothing within me had changed. I didn't even know what I should be feeling, but surely something? I think this was the inception of my quest for a higher connection and meaning. Something wholly experiential. I would continue to seek this for years through my experiences with books, people, music, and art. I never knew what I sought in the world was within me the whole time. It is within each of us. The connection to higher self or the divine is an internal journey through soul to spirit.

What is the Spirit? Is it different from the Soul? I researched several spiritual/religious traditions with this very question in mind. Sometimes both words seem to be interchangeable. In Christianity, the two are sometimes distinguished in meaning. The soul is tied to earthly life. A soul may refer to a person, a human life. A spirit connotes a non-physical being such as an angel. In other parts of the bible, spirit and soul appear to be synonyms.

I have heard reference to the Holy Spirit, one is one of the three entities that comprise the Holy Trinity—The Father, The Son, and the Holy Ghost, or Spirit. Each is considered a facet of God. "A member of the Godhead, the Holy Spirit had no beginning and has no end. With the Father and Son, he existed before creation. The Spirit dwells in heaven but also on Earth in the heart of every believer." For Christians, the Spirit is our direct connection to a higher power or God.[1]

In Hinduism, there is the atman. This equates to the individual eternal soul that goes through birth, death, and rebirth until it achieves enlightenment or moksha. Paramahamsa Sri Swami Vishwananda states that the human soul is covered by "layers of shade." We experience the Soul as the non-physical, intangible something within us. The shade is all the social, tribal conditioning we receive and adopt from the moment we are born. It is the karma or attributes we take on through our experience, through our thoughts, behaviors, and actions.[2]

When the Soul is covered, it is hidden. We are unable to perceive it or consciously connect with the Soul until these layers are removed. Once fully visible, the individual Soul conveys the pure universal Spirit that permeates the entire universe. One may equate the Spirit with the divine or highest (God) consciousness. The Soul is bound by karma, the Spirit is not. The evolution of an individual's Soul consciousness is the process of enlightenment to meet with the Divine.

Many major religious or spiritual traditions such as Christianity, Judaism, Islam, and Hinduism distinguish the soul as that pertaining to the individual and the spirit as universal consciousness that connects to higher power. Most religions today believe in the existence of a soul that lives on after the death of the body.[3] This notion is shared by

Buddhism, Judaism, Zoroastrianism, Islam, and the Bahá'í faith, as well as the belief systems of indigenous cultures of Africa and the Americas.

Just as an empty or negative space can only be described in relation to another visible entity or an object in space, the lack of belief in a faith is similarly described in opposition to other belief systems. Atheists state that there is no God or higher power. After we die, there is no part of ourselves that lives on. Although atheists may agree that humans are conscious beings, they are quite varied in their philosophies. For example, of American atheists, 98 percent state that religion is not important to them, 79 percent say they sometimes feel a sense of awe about the universe, and 36 percent express feeling spiritual well-being at times.[4]

When the subject of consciousness is discussed, it is difficult to explain via an atheist lack of belief system. It is challenging to communicate consciousness and its relationship to Spirit, as I define it. I strive in this book to determine a secular definition of soul and spirit, and respectively regard each as the energy of a sentient being and the energy of the universe that surrounds and connects them.

One might say that Spirit is what animates a person, plant, or animal, and makes it a sentient being. Here I am using spirit as interchangeable with soul. Perhaps all living things are conscious and have within them an innate desire to survive. A lizard is sentient in that it has a certain amount of awareness of itself, surroundings, and other living things. So, is the lizard conscious, and does it have a spirit?

Animism

Animism is the belief that everything in nature has a spirit, whether plant, animal, rock, river, or weather. Animism incorporates a relational worldview in which everything in the universe is infused with anima, or spirit, and the planet is a living, dynamic, interconnected web.[5] This can extend to inanimate objects like buildings, cars, computers, or teddy bears. Animism is woven into popular stories and movies such as *Toy Story* or the *Velveteen Rabbit*, in which toys are living beings with their own motivations, feelings, desires, and spirit.

Whether as the essence or soul of a person, as a nonphysical being, or as the anima that infuses all material objects, Spirit is a unifying force that connects all. Collective Spirit arises from the interrelation of individual spirits or souls that comprise the collective. It is a bond of shared thoughts, feelings, and experiences. This allows us to relate to and understand another human on the other side of the world with a different language, culture, and upbringing, who loves and values life as we do.

Throughout history, humans formed tribes for security and protection. They relied on collective spirit to unify them. They formed belief systems to both explain the meaning of their lives and to ensure the group remained a cohesive tribe.

Forgetting that the whole of Humanity contains a unifying Collective Spirit, and that Collective Spirit extends to all living things on the planet, people readily see differences between themselves and others. "That tribe is not my tribe," they might think, or "Humans are superior to all other living beings."

Problems arise when a group chooses to "other" another group, to disrespect and undermine them. Spirit is a powerful energy, fundamental to every life and perhaps all matter. Perhaps it is time we reestablish Spirit in our lives and elevate its value for us as a connection to higher consciousness and a unifying force.

Heart is intrinsic to the power of our Spirit. The term "from the heart" or "from the bottom of my heart" refers to our deepest and most authentic feelings. The heart represents purity, sincerity, and love. When we are heart-centered, we live our truth with discipline and compassion. This reflects our earthly Spirit or Soul.

When one's Spirit is aligned with their higher self, connected to divine energy, then one lives from the heart, and their thoughts and actions reflect this. If every human became truly heart-centered and compassionate, the collective Spirit of humanity would undergo a massive shift. Priorities and systems would change because we would consciously choose to change them, and we might truly end wars, suffering, pollution, and the degradation of the planet.

Spirit is a pivotal force for humanity's evolution into an enlightened species, one that abhors violence, one that emphasizes unity over separation, one that makes love central to everything it does. It is the compass that can steer humanity's efforts away from exploitation, competition, and greed, and guide it toward cooperation, compassion, and peace.

When Spirit aligns with Mind and Body, we can create tremendous positive change in the world and within ourselves.

Fully aligned people can restructure our economic and political systems, create zero waste solutions, reverse global warming, and end poverty and anguish. All of that and much more is entirely possible. In the next chapter we will explore what is your authentic self.

CHAPTER 9 REFLECTIONS

Your mental thoughts are often much louder than the subtle messages from your soul. What is the difference between a thought that prompts you to take a certain action and a soul calling? We often give all our attention to the mind and think our way logically to a decision. This has its place and time. However, there are moments it may be beneficial to "feel into" a deeper reason to do something. Perhaps it feels like a gentle tug, a persistent disquiet, or an unsettled feeling at the thought of listening to what your mind recommends, when something within is pointing you in another direction. As an example, what that may look like is letting go of a relationship that you have invested time, money, and effort into, in favor of following a calling from the heart that resonates deeply within you, and asks you to move on from that dynamic.

1. Journal prompt: What are your beliefs about your soul or spirit?

2. What do you do to feel connection to the collective spirit? Think of when you felt a disconnection. What did you do as a result? What was your soul hoping for in that moment?

3. What does it mean to "follow your heart"? What is an instance when you decided to follow your heart?

Your Authentic Self

In the Dreamworks animated film *Shrek,* Fiona was cursed to become an ogre daily from sunset to sunrise. This was a source of fear and shame for her, as she and her family hid this fact from the world. As an ogre, Fiona simply did not fit the quintessential identity of a princess–beautiful, graceful, and lithe. Denying this true part of herself, meant living an inauthentic life and identity. Everything changes when Fiona meets Shrek. Her decision to very publicly reveal to him her ogre identity occurs at sunset in the church where she is about to be wed to Lord Faquat.

The genius of this storyline occurs when they share "true love's first kiss" which Fiona had always thought would lift her curse forever. Instead she permanently became an ogre, symbolizing her acceptance of her authentic identity. Shrek and Fiona loving each other, and fully accepting their identities shows the importance of being true to oneself for true happiness. These characters understood and embraced the identity of an ogre, even when the people around them didn't accept it. This is not so easily done for the rest of us, where one's authentic identity can become buried under materialism, accolades, and external markers of success.

One's definition of self depends on what they hold in high regard. A materialist may identify with ego, achievements, and acquisitions, e.g., "I am Sam, I have two homes and three cars, I was a collegiate athlete, I have a wife and three kids, I am a CEO of a mid-sized company." The description may be true, and serve to root him squarely in the material world, but who is Sam beyond these external anchors?

Here's another one. "I am Jane, I am a therapist. I help people manage and overcome their trauma." From this, I still don't know enough about who the real, authentic Jane is, other than she helps with mental health. I recently watched a very touching show focused on neurodivergent young adults looking for romantic relationships. One young man introduced himself by name and declared he is here in this life to spread joy. His whole face expressed that joy, and it was contagious. Is one person's identity better or of greater value than the others? In our materialistic landscape, humans may assess a person's value by their financial means or their external power, but what are they without these aspects?

Think about how you describe yourself to others. Here in the United States, we usually go straight to our occupation to describe who we are. "What do you do?" is the typical query upon meeting someone new. When we are stripped of one's job qualifications, marital status, or even general likes and preferences like "I love comedy movies and spending time at the beach," I speculate that we are at a loss about how to identify ourselves. That is the starting point of truly understanding yourself. This will not negate the external identifiers that describe you in this earthly existence. But to know oneself deeply is to step beyond the ego.

Ego demands identity, and that's not a bad thing. We each need a healthy ego to function in the material world. Any sentence you say that includes "I" refers to your ego.[1] As long as we are tied to our physical bodies, a healthy ego is needed to navigate our world and ensure we acquire our basic needs—air, water, food, shelter. Ego promotes our desire for family, careers, money, and achievement. For the most part, that is how human societies have organized themselves. Even a person who is very self-critical or depressed is having an egoic experience—one built on an extreme focus on self.

Spirituality encourages us to extract ourselves from ego's grip and connect with our higher self. The spiritual path is the quest to overcome ego's control of self so that one can connect with something much bigger than the individual self. Why is this an important and desirable goal? A spiritual worldview connects us to others and all living beings, and there is great strength in that. As conscious and self-aware beings, most humans are keenly cognizant of the fragility and the impermanence of life. This vulnerability can make us fearful. Feeling connected to each other and to a "higher energy" can make us feel stronger and less alone, less like tiny specks on a floating blue ball in space.

In light of that insecurity, humans have been striving since the beginning to form groups like families, communities, societies, cultures, races, and countries. We have tried to tether a religious identity to a higher entity (God). Identity means embracing our sense of individual self as part of our collective. However, we have been unable to rid ourselves of the underlying fears and uncertainties of life. Hence, we traumatize, fight, and kill each other in the name of the group to which we have pledged allegiance.

American spiritual teacher and author Gary Zukav writes about five sensory and multi-sensory humans in his books, *Seat of the Soul* and *Universal Human*.[2] He distinguishes between five-sensory humans who have sought to control and conquer others and their material world using external power, and our evolution to multi-sensory humans who embrace what he calls authentic power.

Having authentic power encompasses a reverence for all life, love, and the absence of judgment. This next-level, multi-sensory self values the intention behind an action and chooses healing over harm. Zukav also states one goal in this earth plane is to align one's personality with one's soul, because from that, authentic power may arise. One's personality ends when one's life ends, but the Soul lives on. One's personality reflects what a soul chooses to work on in its earthly lifetime, as can be seen through experiences—both positive and negative.

When we separate Ego from Self, we can focus on the essence of what we are as eternal beings or souls. We are better able to disidentify from the ego trappings of external power in the material world. We can cease trying to control others and competing for resources. We view ourselves as a part of a much larger whole. Our sense of Self can now be about improving well-being for all.

> *"I am convinced that the deepest desire within each of us is to be liberated from the controlling influences of our own psychic madness or patterns of fear. All other things—the disdain of ordinary life, the need to control others rather than be controlled, the craving for material goods as a means of security and protection against the winds of chaos—are external props that serve as substitutes for the real battle, which is the one waged within the individual soul."*
> **—Caroline Myss**

Caroline Myss, author, spiritual teacher, and medical mystic, teaches that the spiritual path is one of alignment of mind, body, heart, and what she refers to as your "interior life."

Our spiritual path is the path of highest potential. It is why we are here, born into this earthly existence. When you align your mind with this spiritual journey, you will be able to live your true purpose. According to Myss, one's biography becomes one's biology. Illnesses in the body are manifestations of energetic blockages that mirror the mental, emotional, and psychic issues experienced by our minds. These blockages are impediments that keep us from living as our authentic selves.

The spiritual author and speaker Michael Singer writes in *The Untethered Soul: The Journey Beyond Yourself* that you are not the voice in your head.[3] This recognition is the beginning of your self-awareness.

> *"Eventually you will see that the real cause of problems is not life itself. It's the commotion the mind makes about life that really causes problems."*
> —**Michael Singer**

Singer states that the best way to understand consciousness is to experience it within yourself. He states that the flow of energy within you is recognized in many spiritual traditions. Whether called Chi in Chinese medicine, Shakti in the yoga tradition, or Spirit in the Christian tradition, these all refer to your life force. Thoughts form in your mind. Are *you* these thoughts? Or are you the observer of the thoughts, the Self?

Once you recognize the distinction between the mind's thoughts and emotions, and the Self who is the observer of the mind, then it is possible to liberate your soul self from the trappings of the mind.

Our minds tend to cycle through neurotic thoughts and fears, put up walls around negative emotions that lead to energetic blockages, or highjack our peace of mind on a whim. To be the observer of all this is to no longer be tossed around in the often tumultuous ocean of the mind. As the observer, you are fully aware and conscious—you are The Awakened Self.

Singer makes the distinction that the consciousness you experience is of your mental model of reality, not reality itself. You re-create the external world within your mind as you continually narrate this mental model within. You seek to predict future events as a means of controlling them. Singer states that we can quiet the narration of the mind and simply observe our external environment.

To live as one's authentic Self is to stop identifying with the thinking—assessing, judging, complaining, and so on. Can you watch your problematic thoughts flow by objectively and without reaction?

Think of all the times your thoughts have consumed you. Typically, these were not pleasant moments—laying in bed at night, unable to wind down due to the racing, incessant thoughts that keep you awake; trying to focus deeply on one important task while your mind is deluged by a thought parade; endless anxiety that keeps you circling around the same few fears. Striving to connect with your authentic Self will allow you to replace fear with peace, contentment, and love. This is the true nature of the Authentic Self. In the next chapter we will discuss how to nourish your soul.

CHAPTER 10 REFLECTIONS

To know yourself is to understand your motivations, behaviors, beliefs, and values. Some self-reflection is beneficial to understand this. Consider past experiences for examples of when you felt you were the best version of yourself. What thoughts and behaviors were you engaged in that support that desirable version of yourself? Identifying key experiences in your life can help you know yourself better. What about these experiences was so impactful?

Similarly, you can consider significant experiences in which you were not the best version of yourself. What behaviors did you engage in and what were your motivations? Consider what you would do differently if you were to encounter a similar experience.

1. What does it mean to you to align your personality with your soul? What do you need to change to achieve that?

2. What does it mean to you to live at your highest potential? What might you change in your life and within yourself to achieve that?

3. Ask people who know you to describe who you are and reflect on the responses. What is something that wasn't mentioned that you wish was mentioned? What is something that was mentioned that you wish wasn't?

Nourishment of the Soul

We all know of people who have transcended their circumstances and changed the course of their life. These are the individuals who "defy the odds"—surpassing the limitations that they face and succeeding not despite the obstacles, but because of them. Are these extraordinary individuals exclusive to a club that the rest of us "average humans" can't join?

The Spirit of a person is an intangible force that propels them forward even against imperious odds. David Goggins, former Navy Seal, and ultra-endurance athlete, would appear to be a "freak of nature," an extraordinary individual with seemingly superhuman capabilities. Physicist Stephen Hawking, struck with the degenerative disease ALS while still at university at age twenty-two, lived well past the very short lifespan predicted for him, and made immense contributions to his field until his death at age 76. From every corner of the world, there are examples of these individuals who reach extraordinary heights of achievement and overcome their odds. What makes them different from the rest?

There is an element of belief in oneself that is a prerequisite for nourishing the Spirit and setting the stage for an extraordinary life. There are circumstances in life which call for one to be mentally, emotionally, or psychologically strong. Sometimes the Spirit has a central role to play, particularly when the mind is exhausted, and the body is depleted.

One's adversity may be a chronic illness like cancer or autoimmune disease. Chronic illnesses are challenging, and overcoming them must start with a desire and belief that you can do so. Even the strongest desire can waver in the face of repeated or worsening symptoms, reduced quality of life, or chronic pain. To maintain momentum and keep making progress, it is essential to prioritize keeping your spirit up. Spiritual practices such as gratitude and forgiveness helps in this regard and can give you a sense of inner strength and guidance.

Regarding forgiveness, sometime ago, I was speaking with a dear friend I've known since high school. In the process, the subject of forgiveness came up. She had told me a very painful aspect of her past marked by a betrayal by an adult in her childhood. My friend was of the opinion that forgiveness is something one grants to another, and would wonder, "Aren't some things unforgivable?" I agree that her experience was terrible and inexcusable. I proposed to her an alternate understanding of forgiveness–one that is not a "transactional" exchange between people whereby the perpetrator is granted forgiveness for their actions—hopefully in an exchange for a heartfelt apology or a change of attitude or character. Instead, forgiving the other person is all about the victim in the scenario consciously choosing to set aside the emotional and energetic baggage of what was done to her. By releasing this from her being, she is able to lighten the burden for herself, and thereby heal. This can occur whether or not she chooses to verbally tell the person they are forgiven or to accept their apology (should it be given).

Besides forgiveness, here are other spiritual practices you can try:

Purpose - having a connection to something greater than oneself

Resilience - the ability to manage adversity and move forward

Belief - what we hold as true that promotes compassion and mental fortitude

Awe - having a sense of interconnection and positive feelings

Vision - provides resolve, direction, and purpose

Hope - having an optimistic mindset

Service - acts of love, social connection, improves longevity

Create ways you can engage with one or more of these spirit-centered practices, and make them a part of your life. For example, gratitude as a practice may be something good in your daily life you verbally acknowledge or perhaps write about in a daily journal.

Another soul nourishing action is to connect with others who bolster our spirits, and bring warmth and optimism to the conversation. It is no coincidence that people living in one of the blue zones mentioned in Chapter 8 prioritize their social network. If you recall, the blue zones are small regions in the world that have the largest populations of people living over one hundred years. Nurturing relationships not only adds years to one's life, but can be the edge one needs to strive for a healthier and happier outcome.

Whether your challenge in life is your health, finances, safety, or something else, identify the resources that will feed your Spirit. Sometimes that resource is something much, much bigger than you—God, the universe, nature, or something else. Your belief in something far more powerful than you, something that can fortify and help you face adversity, can make all the difference.

Have a positive belief that the improbable is entirely possible, your state of being is mutable, and you have within yourself the resources and grit to change any circumstance.

Here the heart must be mentioned. By heart, I mean the metaphorical central point from which our deepest, most authentic feelings come. We've all heard the expression, "lead with your heart" or "follow your heart." The implication here is that there is some intelligence within us that we can call upon besides that which comes from the mind. Some may call it, intuition.

What are we tapping into when we access our intuition? I believe this is both within our individual being and in the collective consciousness. To tune into one's heart is to align with a higher intelligence, energy, or spirit force, much like resonating frequencies. These moments of alignment may feel timeless and spaceless, and urge you to stay in the present moment, and hold that experience.

It is your heart-centered Spirit self that encourages you to seek out awe and revere life. It is your heart that leads you to make a life decision—such as leaving a job or career that is very lucrative to pursue work that ignites your passion—that your logical, egoic mind may balk at. The Mind can conjure many reasons your soul-centred choice is not a good one. But when your Mind moves out of the way, only then can the Spirit play. This does not mean that Mind and Spirit are mutually exclusive. With true alignment your mind is very in tuned to the spirit's calling and your mental landscape–thoughts, feelings, beliefs–all reflect your soul's deep desires. The soul naturally resonates with the fundamental consciousness all around us.

When you begin to tap into the living consciousness that is all around you, synchronicities become more evident. Synchronicities are defined as signs from the universe that align with your psyche, to which you attribute intuition and emotion.[1] Skeptics may shrug these off and state that all synchronicities are just coincidences. Regardless, these are meaning-making opportunities that can guide you through life, should you choose to embrace them. I challenge you to ask the universe for a sign the next time you have a decision to make or want some guidance, and then be aware and open to receive such signs.

Many people see repeating number patterns, sometimes called angel numbers. "1111" or "111" for example may appear on clocks you happen to glance at, or on a sign or address. This is one phenomenon I regularly encounter. I dismissed it as coincidence for a while before realizing the frequency and timing went far beyond coincidence. I have often thought about a decision I needed to make and pondered whether the path I wanted to take was the right one. Sometimes I'd unconsciously glance at my watch or phone and I'd see "11:11" and have a sense that I was heading in the right direction.

Whether you are a true believer in synchronicities or not, or you believe in any other metaphysical pursuits like aura reading, psychic abilities, astrology, or tarot, give yourself some space to experience astonishment when a synchronicity shakes up your world. Suspend judgment, seek out one or more of these interesting practices, and give it a try. Of course, filter your experiences through your own intuition and feeling states when assessing what something means for you.

It is not far-fetched to think that we and everything in our conscious planet and universe pulsates with energy.

Everything is Energy

"Everything is energy, and that is all there is to it. Match the frequency of the reality you want, and you cannot help but get that reality. It can be no other way. This is not philosophy. This is physics."
—*Albert Einstein*

Because I am a holistic health coach, and particularly a functional medicine-trained coach, I look at the human body as a collection of interconnected systems. I include in this framework the energetic system that is treated in energy medicine. This system affects the other systems of the body, but for the purpose of discussion, let's consider energy alone.

Each of us has an energy field that permeates around and through us. In metaphysical circles, this is called the aura. These days one can't throw a rock without hitting some information on chakras, chakra healing, or chakra cleansing. The science of chakras originated from ancient India and is thousands of years old. Both Hinduism and Buddhism incorporate the concept of energy centers (chakras) throughout the body.

These energy centers are connected throughout the body via energy channels. The seven primary chakras in Hinduism are found along one's spine from base to the top of the head. Hinduism accounts for many more minor chakras as well.[2] Many in the Western world have come to embrace the seven-chakra system and attribute a specific color to each so that they align with the seven visible colors of the rainbow: red, orange, yellow, green, blue, indigo, and violet.

Another millennia-old system of healing we have mentioned before is Traditional Chinese Medicine (TCM). TCM has at its core, the concept of energy channels called meridians that run throughout and around the body. The energy life force is called chi or qi. All healing modalities within TCM focus on balance and equilibrium throughout the body. Some of these modalities include acupuncture/acupressure, Tui Na (massage), cupping, herbal medicine, Tai Chi, and Qi Gong. Each of these methods of treatment involve the balance of energy and release of stagnant energy.[3]

Ancient cultures have known for a very long time that we are made of both matter and energy, tangible, physical parts and intangible, invisible parts. To simply study the workings of the material parts of our body leaves us with an incomplete model. The current practice of allopathic medicine does not incorporate the energy system.

The energy system of the body includes invisible forces interacting with other invisible forces. Our energy system influences and impacts the material system.[4] We in the West try to explain consciousness through material changes in the brain. Of course, we've come up short—consciousness simply cannot be explained through a materialist lens.

There are many energy-based healing systems that are now being acknowledged and incorporated into complementary care within allopathic medicine, such as reiki and craniosacral therapy, acupuncture, acupressure, and ayurveda.[5] Recently, there has been a resurgence of ancient healing techniques, perhaps, because we are finding that many of our complex, chronic diseases can't be adequately treated using the pills and techniques of traditional medicine, and we recognize more and more the need to nourish the spirit to enhance life and health.

As energy medicine expert Donna Eden writes in her book, *Energy Medicine: Balancing Your Body's Energies for Optimal Health, Joy, and Vitality*:

> "Your body is, in fact, a cascading fountain of energy systems, remarkably complex, exquisitely coordinated, and entirely unique" [pg 35].

We can benefit from a little more lightness of being in our lives. As medical mystic Caroline Myss writes, "The more history you have, the denser your body. "This correlates with what the scientist, author, and speaker Joe Dispenza says about the three-dimensional world we all inhabit. He explains that it is an illusion. Anything we want or desire in our material world requires us to use matter to move matter through space, so as to make that desire a reality. It takes time and energy, and it is cumbersome.[6]

How does one shorten the distance between cause and effect? He explains that different rules apply. One must create in the quantum field, which is outside of 3D space and time. This is the energetic field that creates matter. In Dispenza's quantum model, thoughts become things when a person's energy is fully coherent in mind, body, and clear intention. They are in a state of what he calls "elevated emotions" or "heart coherence." Whether you are a skeptic inclined to dismiss these principles as pseudoscience, or you are a true believer in the methodology, his studies and data show the success of his methods, and there is something to the idea of harnessing one's energy to manifest a desired reality.

We know from quantum physics that there is a dual nature to light—namely that a photon can be either a wave or a particle. In Deepak Chopra's book *Quantum Body, How Our Thoughts and Emotions Influence Us and the World*, Chopra states that thoughts and emotions influence gene activity through the Hypothalamic Pituitary Axis (HPA), which regulates the body's stress response. When stressed, the body releases hormones such as adrenaline and cortisol, that can alter gene expression.[7]

Genes can be turned on or off. Through a series of processes that Chopra covers in his book, thoughts become "things" in the body, and the body's state is changed. He correlates between mental activity and quantum states, whereby emotions impact through epigenetics. Is it possible that we can create quantum therapies to help heal people's adverse mental states and suffering? We have a ways to go, but I believe we will get there.

To nourish the Spirit is to recognize that we are energetic beings choosing to have an earthly experience. In the next chapters, the importance and influence of space on well-being is described. The negative impacts of how we have treated our spaces, why space is an important dynamic on the Well-being Pyramid, and how to nourish our spaces is discussed in Part 4 of *The Aligned Human*.

CHAPTER 11 REFLECTIONS

The impact of emotions on one's mental and physical states is undeniable. If we get angry, our face may turn red. An acute episode of stress may cause us to sweat profusely. We may experience fear as a dry mouth sensation. Prolonged or repeated experiences can have a lasting influence on health and well-being. Optimizing modifiable lifestyle factors such as exercise, nutrition, sleep, stress, and relationships will positively impact your well-being and can help mitigate the damaging outcomes of strong emotions by supporting a more resilient mind and body .

1. What spiritual practices (gratitude, forgiveness, purpose, resilience, belief, awe, vision, hope, service) resonate most with you? What new practice will you try going forward?

2. How do you interact with the Universe? What signs or synchronicities do you receive or have you received in response to a question?

3. Make a list of your habits that have a negative impact and what you experience negatively in each case. What small steps are you willing to take to change that negative habit using modifiable lifestyle factors?

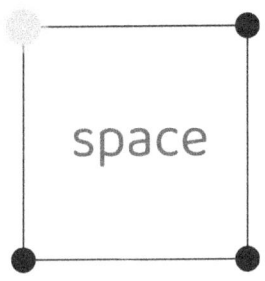

Part 4

Two weeks ago I ran down these stairs.
Standing unsteadily at the base, returned after inpatient treatment
One flight seems unsurmountable.
So tired and I have not begun to climb.
Step with left and drag right leg up to meet it.
One down, seventeen to go I think.
Frustration tears mixed with a bit of self-pity.
This is my home, my space.
Now I cautiously navigate it with a disability.
We have a new relationship, this space and I.
I no longer take it for granted.
My space will not allow me to give up.
Every step is now a triumph.
Every win is a reminder that I am still here.

CHAPTER 12

Triggers and Environmental Toxicity

I have never felt more at peace and oneness with the Universe than when I am in a warm ocean, swimming amidst a plethora of ocean life. Within the space of the ocean, time is suspended, the silence stills any frazzled nerves, and the graceful creatures around me remind me that there are spaces within time when I am aligned with Earth and fully immersed in its best.

A while ago, I had the exciting opportunity to snorkel at night with manta rays. I was with a few others in the water with snorkel gear, holding the side of a floatation device. We were instructed to lay very still and had foam noodles clasped at the feet to keep our entire body on the surface of the water. No one was allowed to reach out and touch a ray, should they swim by.

Within a few minutes, we could see them approach underneath. Their immense wingspan and rhythmic flapping of fins—that appeared to be in slow motion to me—left me in awe. They continued to swim head to tail with each other in a circular path creating a vortex of sorts. With their mouths opened to full capacity they would feed on volumes of krill and plankton that had risen near the surface.

I had a compelling urge to touch one as she swam too far underneath me to reach with my hand. I was following the rules, and would not have done so had she been close enough to touch. She circled deep underneath and came up closer as she continued the circular path. But this time was different. She came up close and purposefully grazed my forearm with her belly as if in greeting. Joy! In that moment we were just two creatures having an earthly experience in the shared space of the ocean.

Space is very important to human health and well-being. When we think of space, the first thing that comes to mind is outer space—the universe. The second is our physical environment here on earth. Let us discuss the latter in this chapter. We take great care of our spaces and even revere them, as in the case of holy lands, and manmade structures we consider sacred, such as mosques, temples, gurdwaras, monasteries, churches, and synagogues.

There are natural spaces, such as Kashi in Northern India or the Camino del Santiago in Spain that we revere due to the symbolic meanings we give them. We love nature, and most of us seek to be immersed in it to experience the awe of the natural world. Northern California, where I live, is known for its majestic redwood forests. It's spectacular and awe-inspiring to look up the giant trunk of a two hundred foot coastal redwood.

Paradoxically, although we seek to preserve the natural world, revere it, and recognize the vital importance of nature to our well-being, we continue to systematically destroy it. As a collective, we pollute and degrade the land, depleting it of the very nutrients our food supply and our health depends on. It seems we are both reverent of our connection to nature and fearful of our dependence on it. That fear and insecurity perhaps makes us squander our natural resources in an attempt to assuage this insecurity and feel in control.

This complex relationship with nature—marked by both reverence and reckless exploitation—has profound consequences not only for the planet, but for ourselves. How we treat the earth is mirrored in the quality of the food it yields, and ultimately, in the state of our own health.

We are what we eat. Our health and the health of the planet cannot be separated from each other. Any non-packaged whole food can be traced to the earth on which it was grown. Every food we consume has a story, a history. When you eat it, it becomes a part of you. Buy, cook, and eat more whole foods. Become deeply aware of what you are putting in your body. You can even grow your own food—there is no better way to establish a very visceral, first hand connection to food than to do this.

"When you eat, you take in a part of the earth. How we treat the planet is how we treat our own bodies."
—**Sadhguru**

What one eats or doesn't eat is very important, but not just in a manner that's limited to individual diet. Food choices, availability, affordability, politics, and industry have large-scale effects on the health and well-being of all of us and the planet.

Dr. Mark Hyman is one of the most widely known functional medicine practitioners who focuses on a food-as-medicine approach to health. In his book, *Food Fix: How to Save Our Health, Our Economy, Our Communities, and Our Planet—One Bite at a Time* Dr. Hyman draws a parallel between how we feed our bodies and how we treat the planet.[1] He connects the dots from the food on our plate to the intricacies of the food system. Dr. Hyman argues that the food system—how we grow, produce, distribute, consume, and waste it—is the convergence point of human health, as well as environmental and climate health. As we are depleting the earth, so too are we depleting our health.

Humans are increasingly becoming sicker, a sign that we're undermining our own well-being. We are quickly stripping away the life-giving and sustaining resources of the earth. The World Health Organization (WHO) states that climate change is the biggest threat facing human health. They also outline climate change impacts to health that include extreme weather events causing injury and death, illnesses stemming from excessive heat, respiratory illnesses, water, vectors (parasites, viruses, and bacteria), food-borne illnesses, mental health issues, and non-communicable diseases such as autoimmune disease.[2]

A June 2023 CNBC news article states that the United Nations is warning that we have less than sixty years to regenerate our soil, otherwise we will encounter "catastrophic effects."[3] This is due to the damage done from overuse, needlessly cutting down large areas of trees, and abusing the land, all in the interest of supporting the destructive practices implemented to support the manufactured foods to which we are addicted.[4]

Foods such as industrial meat, the soybean and palm oil used in a multitude of processed foods (start reading every label of food products to see how pervasive this is), bottled mineral water, and cereal crops are each choices we have made. Soil is the microbiome of the earth. As we deplete the biodiversity, mineral-richness, and regenerative ability of the earth, we do the same to our own microbiomes.

The standard western diet of ultra-processed packaged foods, refined carbohydrates, and high sugar is largely responsible for the diminishing of diversity in our gut microbiota.[5] The microbes in our GI tract and on our skin are also in our environment. If the environment that sustains us is compromised, human health is compromised too.

We may feel we are an insignificant endpoint of a complicated food system that Dr. Hyman states is broken. But if that is the case, how can change happen? We are the billions of consumers of the food that is produced. Each of us can make individual food choices that collectively make an impact on the industry.

We can educate ourselves and communicate our desire for improvements. We can support the organizations striving to make impactful changes to farming practices. We can demand for that change to happen now.

There are environmental toxins that can drive some complex chronic conditions like autoimmune illnesses. According to the Global Autoimmune Institute, up to 70 percent of these diseases may be driven by harmful substances in the environment.[6] Toxic chemicals such as metals, pollutants, and other substances that disrupt the immune and endocrine systems are found in the air, water, and soil.[7]

Heavy metals such as mercury, lead, chromium, cadmium, and arsenic have been linked to autoimmune diseases, especially those involving the thyroid such as Hashimoto's or Graves' disease.[8] More than 12 percent of Americans have thyroid disease and about 60 percent are not even aware of it.[9] Heavy metals can toxify organs such as the kidney and liver. Other environmental toxins and pollution can cause respiratory illnesses, asthma, and cancer.

Toxic-Free Future (toxicfreefuture.org) a national organization whose mission is research and advocacy for the health of the environment, report that mercury is introduced to the air and our food and water systems by coal-burning plants, oil refineries, dental offices (amalgam fillings), and cremation facilities. It is also in fluorescent light bulbs and thermometers. Discarded mercury gets into the water and contaminates fish, which humans then eat.

In a podcast episode of the Doctor's Farmacy, Dr. Mark Hyman and Dr. Elizabeth Boham discuss heavy metal toxicity and the functional medicine approach to assessing toxic load in a patient as well as detoxifying the body.[10] The doctors mention that often when one is not getting any better from chronic conditions despite much testing, heavy metals may be the culprit.

Lead is stored in the bones and organs. Although it was removed from paint in 1978, some old pipes are still lead-based. These heavy metals can create antibodies against the healthy tissue in the body which can lead to autoimmune illnesses. One may have stored and accumulated a toxic load over their lifetimes and these heavy metals will remain deposited.

Eliminating them from the body requires a specific treatment called chelation. Substances called chelators are introduced to bind to the heavy metals and transport them out of the body. Dr. Hyman makes the interesting point that checking for heavy metals is a "massive blind spot" in the practice of western medicine.[11]

It has been documented in patients with kidney disease that by chelating the lead from the body it reversed the kidney disease and prevented the need for dialysis. Yet, western medicine is not checking for chronic heavy metal toxicity as a standard of care. Wouldn't it be better to not have to care for a sick human who has been exposed to a toxin by better caring for our spaces and eliminating harmful substances?

There is increasing consumer awareness of the need to address our climate issues. Thirty-two percent of consumers make this a criterion in their purchases and support of goods. However, the consumer must be discerning about the quality of those goods, and the authenticity of the brand's claims, particularly in the light of cases of *greenwashing*. Greenwashing is a false representation of a product as being eco-conscious. It is an insidious and manipulative ploy to trick a consumer into thinking that when they purchase a particular product, it is sustainable, eco-friendly, and helping the environment.[12]

Greenwashed consumers are inundated with product advertising that includes the word "natural" and is significantly green in color. As a thorough reader of labels, largely out of necessity, I am frustrated that the ingredient "natural flavors" is allowed to be included in food products without openly telling the public what the so-called "natural flavor" is. These products are often more expensive than their traditional counterparts and the marketing approach used is one that preys upon a consumer's emotional affinity to the natural world.

There are many examples of clothing companies that claim their goods are sustainable and fair-trade. But, are their workers treated well and provided safe working conditions? Does their clothing truly address the environmental impact and treat all their workers fairly at every point of their end-to-end production process? Companies that thrive on the *fast fashion* trend tend to provide a negative answer to these questions. Fast fashion is a term that refers to clothing produced very quickly and cheaply, driven by consumer demand for the latest trends. It began around twenty years ago and quickly gained momentum.[13]

Generally, the clothing doesn't last very long and is not intended for long-term use. Fast fashion's goal is to produce products quickly and cheaply. Fair trade is not central to its process. The environmental impact of producing fast fashion is immense. Dyes often contain toxic chemicals like formaldehyde and chromium that are endocrine disruptors.[14] Fast fashion utilizes an enormous amount of water and energy, and the dyes used in textiles pollute our waters.

The fibers from synthetic fabrics contain microplastics that never degrade, and remain in our oceans. The energy costs and pollution from manufacturing these materials is very significant. The cotton used in the creation of these materials is heavily treated with pesticides while being grown.

My own experience with toxic chemicals happened years ago with a blazer and pant suit purchased for an upcoming interview. I wore the suit and later realized my arms and legs were covered with rashes. A trip to the dermatologist did not confirm what this might be, and a core biopsy was taken. It revealed nothing, and about a week after staying away from the offending clothing—I angrily returned it to the store—the rashes went away. I believe there was a dye in the material that triggered my contact dermatitis.

It is important to be an informed consumer. Take a stand against practices that are polluting the planet and our bodies, and impacting human well-being because our lives depend on it. There is no such thing as an "over there" problem, in which it impacts the poor textile worker in another country but has no bearing on the well-being of a consumer in the United States.

This is everyone's problem. Ultimately, we and our planet bear the cost of destructive practices. We are inexorably tied to our physical spaces. We can respect and honor them by restructuring our industries (and end-to-end supply chains) to eliminate waste and pollution. We can utilize AI to address our most pressing climate issues and food quality and scarcity problems, as well as to produce more sustainable materials.

AI and the Environment: The Paradoxical Solution

AI can provide us with a powerful means to combat environmental issues. Paradoxically, our current and proposed AI data centers have a very large environmental footprint.

A February 2024 article on the World Economic Forum website discusses several ways AI is being used to address our environmental issues. These include quantifying the amount of meltwater from icebergs and tracking the speed at which it is happening. With the use of AI and satellite technology, global deforestation and carbon sequestration is being monitored. There are United Nations projects using AI to help vulnerable communities in Africa to improve waste management, track weather patterns and improve clean energy availability.[15] It is encouraging to hear there are projects to improve recycling, ocean clean up, and the decarbonization of oil and gas industries. Clearly AI is already poised to be instrumental in addressing our climate issues.

However, there are challenges to scaling the implementation of AI that concern energy and environmental impact. Just training an AI large language model (LLM) requires immense amounts of electricity (megawatt hours) and emits tons of carbon. Also, considerable amounts of fresh water are required to keep these machines cool. So, the implementation of AI itself is not without substantial environmental impacts which are felt in the regions where these data centers are located.[16]

Fossil fuels, as opposed to carbon-free energy, are often being used simply to handle the power demands associated with training these LLMs, because it is easily accessible in a region. This adds a tremendous amount of air pollution and consumption of fresh water to that geographical area. It is vital that in the expeditious effort to develop viable AI solutions, that this not be a wild grab for energy of any kind and at any cost to a local environment. We must do this right and develop environmentally responsible AI. Let us not fall back to the exploitative practices of the past when it comes to socioeconomically vulnerable populations and the land they claim as home.

Like the phrase, "You have to spend money to make money," the idea of fully sustainable AI seems contradictory, especially at the rapid rate at which it is evolving. It is clear that the use of traditional power plants is not a viable strategy due to greenhouse gas emissions,and the untenable load it puts on the existing power grid . An October 24, 2024 NPR article states that due to the unrelenting demands for power to feed the current growth trajectory of AI, tech companies are looking for reliable alternatives.[17] Even though there is an acknowledgement of the need for renewable resources and a sustainable framework to power AI efforts, there is still an urgency to meet the energy needs right now.

Solar and wind power is used in data centers and geothermal heat is being considered, but for a consistent source that will meet the skyrocketing demands, many tech companies are considering small nuclear reactors (SMRs)—a viable clean energy solution which can use much less water, liquid metal, or molten salt for cooling. But, these designs still produce radioactive waste which must be safely handled to protect human and environmental health.

Whatever we do, we must remain cognizant of our deep-rooted relationship and dependence on the environment that supports us. In our haste to advance and to implement AI solutions (as beneficial as these may be for human well-being), let us not be short-sighted. Ultimately sustainable and renewable energy is the cornerstone of human well-being as well as well-being of the planet. That is not just a data center issue, it is one that encompasses our entire power infrastructure that still relies on fossil fuels to generate power. Perhaps AI's soaring demand for more power and the tech industry's scramble to meet those demands presents an opportunity for a surge in newer solutions that can better enable all our power needs than natural gas. And that could be a win-win for human well-being. We take a look in the next chapter at our metaphorical relationship to space and its impact to human well-being.

CHAPTER 12 REFLECTIONS

Cutting down or even eliminating ultra processed food from your diet can be difficult. Perhaps you have some go-to snacks such as Reese's peanut butter cups or Flamin Hot Cheetos that you love and crave. You know they have no nutritional benefit and probably have some harmful chemical ingredients as well. Education is everything. The cheetos contain MSG and the food dyes Red 40, Yellow 6, and Yellow 5. The peanut butter cups have the preservative TBHQ, which is associated with an increased risk of cancer, food allergies, and also neurotoxic effects from regular ingestion.[18] How will you go about choosing healthier options?

1. What are your sacred spaces? How do these spaces enhance your well-being? Visit your chosen sacred space, or create one for yourself. This could be a corner of your home or perhaps a room or garden. Sit in stillness and take note of the sensations that arise. Do you feel your heart expanding? Are you more grounded?

2. As a challenge, spend one entire day only eating whole non-packaged foods. Track the sources of each food, e.g., what is the geographic origin of the banana you ate? Was it organic? If not, what pesticides were used on the banana and for what purpose?

3. Download the Yuka or BobbyApproved app and use it to scan the bar codes of items you regularly buy as you peruse the grocery store isles. What packaged food product contained harmful ingredients, and what were those ingredients?

4. Research the end-to-end process of your favorite sustainable and ethical fashion brand. Is it truly a clean product? Are all workers in the supply chain of that product treated fairly? Does their work on the product expose them to any toxicity? Are they fairly compensated for their work?

Space as a Mental Construct

"What haunts me is not exactly the absence of literal space so much as a deep craving for metaphorical space: release, escape, some kind of open-ended freedom."
—Naomi Klein

Space as the fourth dynamic on the Well-being Pyramid represents its complex relationship with human well-being. This chapter discusses some examples of what is meant by space.

Space is Between Objects

Our physical experience is what is tangible to us. What we can see, hear, touch, taste, and smell, we equate with reality. Thus, it makes sense that our focus is on objects—a chair, car, house, trees, or a person. But our perception of the physical as reality doesn't excuse the fact that a nonphysical space simultaneously exists around our 'real' objects. Such has been the design of our existence.

When you study design, you learn to pay attention to negative space, or whitespace, as it is known in the discipline. Negative space is just as much a design element of a layout as the objects. You learn to play with negative space by using it to draw the eye toward the important elements and to give your vision a place to "rest."

Whitespace incorporated into text allows for easier reading. Google's main search page is mostly whitespace, by design, with the goal of having the eye go directly to the most important element—the search bar. Subconsciously, the viewer experiences a sense of calm from the lack of aesthetic pollution while they interact with the search bar.

Space is Silence and Time

Perhaps the same applies to our experience of space, on both the mental and physical levels. We equate space with time. In that sense, asking someone to give you some space is a request for physical space, but also for time. Having the "space" to ponder means having the time to do so. Many places of worship feature only the sounds of ordered chanting, singing, bells, and gongs.

"Between stimulus and response there is a space. In that space is our power to choose our response. In our response lies our growth and our freedom."
—Viktor E. Frankl

Space is an opportunity to gain wisdom and clarity. Sometimes, we feel we are hurtling through space and time, striving to meet the needs of family, work, and everything else. Taking a sabbatical from work opens more space to recoup, re-evaluate, and reconnect. As an antidote to burn out, some employers are granting sabbatical time to their employees. Some employees even take sabbaticals without pay.

A February 22, 2023, article in the *Harvard Business Review* reports that the number of workers utilizing sabbaticals has risen.[1] In a study of fifty interviewees, most people experienced positive effects from time off from work. They returned to their workplaces with a deeper connection to themselves—their own intuition and creativity. It was often an opportunity to shed the professional "box" within which they operated, for a less regimented life. It was the opportunity to ask the deeper questions of "who am I really?" and "what do I want my work to be?" For many, it injected new enthusiasm into the jobs they had.

Space is not Empty

Everything in and on our planet is made of atoms—*everything*. At the atomic level, there is mostly space between the nucleus and the electrons that surround it. Since an atom is 99.999 percent space, by extrapolation, so are we.[2] The concept of space gets much trickier on the subatomic level, in which electrons move around the nucleus in an electronic cloud that is both wave and particle, spreading with fuzzy probabilities of location.

Even outer space is not an empty void. Most of the known Universe (more than two thirds) is dark energy. About another twenty-five percent is dark matter. That leaves a minuscule five percent or so of known matter like stars, neutrinos, etc.[3] Dark energy is considered the intrinsic energy responsible for the ongoing expansion of our universe. Dark matter is invisible but we know it has mass, and is believed to hold galaxies together. Newer research seems to indicate that dark energy evolves over time.[4] If indeed the rate of expansion of the universe is changing over time, this has some significant implications for the future of our universe. Understanding the nature of the universe's dark energy in space is of great interest to physicists all around the world, as humanity's destiny is tied to it.

Space is Value and Meaning

The meaning we assign to space is subjective. A group of people can see a rainforest and cherish its biodiversity, its ability to purify the air we breathe, and view it as a home for thousands of living beings. Another group can view the rainforest as lucrative land with timber to be cut down and sold. In a similar comparison, one farmer can own acres of land and decide to grow monocrops year after year, stripping the earth until the soil is devoid of nutrients. Another farmer can own land and create a lush, biodiverse, self-sustaining, and regenerative space that provides food and habitat for years to come.

The problem arises when you equate your ownership of that space with the freedom and choice to do anything you wish with it, without consideration for how those choices may impact the well-being of other entities who either depend on the space or are inadvertently affected by the negative consequences of your choices.

If you live in a high-rise apartment building, as I did decades ago while schooling in Center City Philadelphia, then you consider the confines of your apartment as your space. Anyone or anything dictating how you may live in that space, what you can or can't do, can feel like an intrusion. Yet, the apartment building is itself an ecosystem—an ecosystem of humans. There are the obvious shared resources like utilities, laundry, water, electricity, and common areas. There is also the less acknowledged shared space of the ventilation system. One person's choice to smoke within their apartment does not guarantee the smoke stays confined to their apartment. The smoke may travel through the vents into another apartment and impact others as secondhand smoke. Also, noise from one apartment will likely be heard in another apartment.

So, to designate ownership of space, we also impose boundaries on spaces. Space is also commodified within our economic system, its value depending on supply and demand, as do all goods and services. We may give a space a higher value because the supply is limited, such as an oceanfront property. That property is coveted (demand is higher) due to its proximity to something that is mutually agreed upon as desirable—the beach.

Space as a Digital Environment

Imagination, technology, and collective human innovation has brought us the Internet we know today. Cyberspace has become as real to most of us as our physical, tangible environments. The entire world, the human collective, is linked through interconnected networks across the planet and via satellites in space.

I am old enough to remember the birth of the internet for public use—Web 1.0 and then the 2.0 version we have right now. The elegance of this distributed computing framework is extraordinary, second only to the evolution of human adoption of the internet for a myriad of purposes. We connect, sell, buy, display, disseminate information, entertain, research, trade, and date in this invisible space.

The next version of our internet, Web 3.0, is more immersive: an intersection of augmented and virtual reality with artificial intelligence. The intention is for this to be a truly decentralized platform using blockchain technology as the backbone for a new fully digital economy.[5] As disruptive as Web 2.0 has been to many industries, Web 3.0 seems poised to do much more.

The multidimensional nature of the metaverse, driven by a company like Meta, allows the end user to feel as if they are in and immersed in a separate space. The metaverse, like any other technology, is not inherently good or bad—it's simply a tool. How we utilize it is the determining factor for its impact on us.

As much as the web can be a place to exploit, undermine, and prey upon others, it can also be a space for gathering and connection, where human consciousness is raised. Our digital space has a pivotal role to play now and in our future.

We are interconnected at a speed and level that has never existed before, and this presents an opportunity to increase compassion, cooperation, and care for one another. We must move beyond the profit-driven, exploitative nature of our legacy systems to restructure how we do business, live life, and care for each other. In the final chapter of Part 4, Space, we will discuss how we nourish our spaces.

CHAPTER 13 REFLECTIONS

Space is becoming even more important to us in the current age. I was recently in New York City, navigating the streets and the subway system from midtown to uptown to downtown. I hadn't visited in many years, and the lack of space around me was quite jarring at first. I was navigating through crowds where the people were well within my usual radius of comfortable distance. Everywhere around me, I was sharing space with multitudes of strangers, making an effort not to bump into anyone else.

It made me wonder how the native New Yorkers decompress and relax. Perhaps their personal living spaces are their sanctuaries, places of reprieve. When I looked at the faces of the strangers I passed, they didn't seem overly stressed out, as far as I could tell. They seemed to flow with the rhythm and pulse of the city. So space and what it means to the individual is subjective. Some love the bustle and noise of people all around them. They find it enlivening and stimulating. Consider the spaces you regularly navigate and understand what draws you to them or what repels you.

1. Describe the last time you took space for yourself. How long did that last and what changed in your daily routine? How did taking time and space for yourself benefit your well-being?

2. Consider the spaces within which you live, work, and play as ecosystems. In each case, what objects, people, or living entities do you depend on for well-being in that ecosystem? What depends on you?

3. What is the digital space to which you claim ownership or perhaps to which you feel you belong? If you have a website, or social media platform, how do you care for that digital space and the people interacting with it? How does that space impact your mental well-being?

Nourishment of Space

The psychology of color is fascinating. At a color theory class I took at UCLA years ago, one of the many exercises we had to do using acrylics was to paint a specific mood. I divided a large sheet of canvas paper into eight quadrants and repeated the same pencil drawing of a bedroom with a bed, lamp, and dresser in each quadrant. I started with blue paint, then tinted it with varying amounts of white paint to create four different shades of blue. I then used more blue paint and shaded it with varying amounts of black paint to create a few more dark shades of blue. I used some of the more subdued shades of blue to paint the bedroom scene in the first quadrant. That scene represented sadness.

I executed a similar set of steps with the lighter shades of blue in the next quadrant to represent calmness or tranquility. What I found fascinating was that two very different moods had been captured for the same space using one base color of blue paint. I did the same exercise with yellow, with one quadrant representing happiness and another showing anxiety. It was interesting to note the spectrum of emotions that could be evoked with a single color.

Color does more than just influence mood. For example, surgical scrubs are green because green is opposite red on the color wheel. The scrubs were made green to contrast with the red of blood and tissue. The green color provided some relief to the eyes, reduced eye strain, and allowed the surgeon to better distinguish between shades of red in surgery.

Color choices for a room can add visual interest and vibrancy. Using a "pop" of color breathes life into a space. If you are not someone who incorporates many colors in your spaces, search for "colorful room aesthetic" on the internet to understand what I mean. The bright, saturated colors seem to add energy to the space. Psychologically, that energy is stimulating and can uplift your mood.

How we cultivate our living spaces reveals the connection we have to our environment. Interior design has been an intrinsic element of how we build and set up our spaces since the beginning of civilization. We only began to recognize it as its own discipline in the late nineteenth century.[1] However, evidence of the care and consideration that has always gone into the creation of interior space can be found in ancient ruins worldwide.

Derinkuyu, located in modern day Turkey, is the largest subterranean city, and housed over two thousand people! Derinkuyu descends eighteen stories underground and was designed with ventilation, light, and water access.[2] This space was made to hide its people from invaders on land, and was predominantly used from 780 A.D. to 1180 A.D.[3] It sheltered, protected, and provided for an entire city. It is mind boggling to think of how Derikuyu was first conceived as an idea and then successfully implemented as a space.

Humans have created dwelling spaces by utilizing natural resources in a multitude of ways, with an eye for functionality, form, and beauty. People have understood that the spaces they create have energy and impact on those who enter. This is exemplified by the ancient Chinese art of Feng Shui, which originated approximately six thousand years ago.

Feng Shui is centered around five elements—water, wood, earth, fire, and metal. The core philosophy of Feng Shui is to live in harmony with one's environment, and to position ourselves and our things to optimize our lives. The placement of a chair, or bed, or the way chi can circulate through the house are some considerations that are made. These principles were originally applied to exterior environments. People would observe the wind direction, and position their spaces near waterways, or at the feet of mountains and hills that provided protection.[4] Taoist principles, which underlie Feng Shui, are part of a larger philosophy of "harmonic order of nature and society" that encompasses all aspects of life.[5]

Everything from the direction the doors face, to slanted walls and sharp corners that do not allow the chi to circulate, are considered while designing a space, as well as colors, lighting, and the impact on our five senses. There is so much thought that goes into the design of a space, including purpose, balance, proportion, traffic or flow through the room.

The practice of space clearing has also been used in many different cultures and traditions as a way to nourish the space so that it may nourish its inhabitants. There is angelic space clearing, which calls upon angels such as Michael or Gabriel to support and assist in creating harmony for the home. The ancient Druids of Celtic society had their own space-purifying ritual, utilizing oak and mistletoe, which they considered sacred. Native Americans have shamanic rituals for the same purpose. Shamans utilize sacred herbs such as sage, sweetgrass, cedar, and tobacco.

Hindus perform specific rituals for a new space before they move into it. In my cultural tradition of birth, we place a small statue or picture of the deity Lord Ganesha (the elephant-headed god of auspicious new beginnings) in the home and heat milk on the new stove until it boils over. This gesture is a symbol of overflowing prosperity to come. People typically burn incense to purify the air. These practices originate from the ancient Indian Vedic system and Hindu culture.

The idea of nurturing a space so that it can nourish us is universal. We experience it when we go to a spa that is designed to appeal to all our senses. The space is peaceful, often with earthy colors and lots of plants. We see a space that makes us feel cared for and relaxed. We hear the soothing sounds of instrumental ambient music, smell the fragrances of the air and the massage oils, we experience therapeutic touch via massage, and we taste the delicious cup of tea we are given before or after our experience. Going to a spa is equated with self-care, taking the time to slow down and just be in the present moment and space. There is a feeling of being held by the space.

The spaces we cultivate are often a gathering place for friends, family, and like-minded groups. Early in human history, we realized that it is to our advantage to form these cooperative groups where we can learn from each other and work together. This led to a "cumulative and non-genetic evolution," through which we learned more rapidly as a community, thus progressing the collective.[6]

Community spaces, both physical and virtual, provide a sense of belonging and a counter to loneliness. Typically, a community will gather and form because of a shared interest. Whether it is a group that lives in a particular neighborhood or has a shared goal, such as an environmental clean-up organization, or shares a love for a particular subject such as books, wine, or sports, communities are diverse and tend to allow people to join regardless of race, religion, gender, or sex. Having a shared space is intrinsic to being a community or tribe. Whether physical or virtual, there must be a meeting place or platform, a "space" that supports connection between its members.

It is when that collective group only allows homogenous members and excludes those not of the same demographic or family that it could rightly be called a tribe. A tribe typically has a deep-rooted connection that is a part of its members' identities.

Humans have formed tribes throughout our history, clustering as small hominid groups. Tribes provided security, protection, and a means of acquiring possessions—even those belonging to another tribe.[7] One can observe how both the benefits and travesties of tribalism have played out in the modern world.

We still have groups of indigenous tribes worldwide who live together peacefully and with reverence and care for the planet. One United Nations statistic states: "There are more than 476 million indigenous people in the world, spread across 90 countries and representing 5,000 different cultures. They make up 6.2 percent of the global population and live in all geographic regions." Indigenous people are three times as likely to live in poverty, their life expectancy is twenty years less than the rest of the worldwide population, and are more likely to die of preventable infectious diseases like malaria and tuberculosis.[8]

Yet, there is a desire in the modern world to learn and adopt the indigenous knowledge of these global community members, in particular the knowledge of how to live in harmony with the biophysical environment. The indigenous populations of today have honed and practiced their ways of living for millennia. There is a great deal of wisdom in these cultures, as well as solutions to the problems of our current times.

Most of our modern medicine and science has come from the knowledge of indigenous people. But often we have exploited them and refused them the benefits of modern healthcare and education. This exploitation continues today, but there are those brave human rights defenders who continue to work tirelessly to help indigenous people in various countries gain rights and equality.

We must expand our definition of community and space to encompass the whole planet and everyone in it. As long as everything and everyone is seen as a means to personal profit, we will continue acting out in violence, manipulation, greed, hatred, and a gross lack of integrity. With these negative drivers impeding the human collective, authentic well-being for each of us and humanity as a whole is firmly out of reach. Authentic well-being starts with an individual's choice and desire to choose better, to do better, and to be better. Let us consider the whole planet as our collective space where humanity communes and bonds. In the next chapter, we will consider the combined influence of mind and body on our well-being.

CHAPTER 14 REFLECTIONS

Think about how you have designed your personal living space, whether it is a house, apartment, condo, or some other structure. What feels comforting, relaxing, or inspiring about it? How functional have you made the space–easy to navigate, easy to find items? How have you used colors, textures, and patterns to appeal to your aesthetics? Tune into the space between objects. What thoughts and emotions are evoked as you contemplate this space? Does it feel safe? Expansive? Stressful? What about your space makes you feel the way you do?

1. What are your top three favorite colors and why do these appeal most to you?

2. Choose a color that you would not normally wear and put that clothing on for a day, e.g., a red shirt. Pay careful attention to how the color makes you feel and act. Notice if you are treated differently by others that day. How did wearing that color make you feel?

3. Our personal spaces are sources of safety and belonging. How do you ensure your space supports your well-being? What are the space-clearing rituals that you practice?

4. Consider a community space to which you belong. What motivates you to go there? What nourishment to your well-being do you receive in that space?

5. What community space do you avoid? What impact does it have on your well-being?

Part 5

Dual Dynamics of the Well-being Pyramid

Self as a teetering sailboat threatening to succumb to the choppy waves.

Acute is an isolated incident. Okay, this happened, not likely to repeat.

Chronic is enduring. Seemingly without end.

My sailboat self perpetually topples

My efforts focus on survival and righting the boat.

Alignment becomes a multi-pronged struggle.

Out of alignment with Mind is anxious, scattered, and restless

Out of alignment with Body is unbalanced, low energy, stuck

Out of alignment with Spirit is disconnected, lonely, numb

Out of alignment with Space is lost, ungrounded, malnourished

In these times I remember…

I carry within me an entire Universe

Ephemeral, interconnected, alive

Feelings as sensations felt in the body

Emotions as thoughts traverse the mind

A divine force animates the spirit

The Earth's frequency, 7.83 Hz, pulsates energy and nourishes my being.

I am mind, sharp and aware
I am body self-healing and intelligent
I am spirit, the heart center of my being
I am space, all that surrounds me both physical and nonphysical

Mind as Air is curious, clever, visionary
Body as Water is fluid, flexible, adaptable
Spirit as Fire is power, transformation, illumination
Space as Earth is expansive, open, limitless

I continue to seek authentic well-being
Alignment of mind, body, spirit, and space
So that I may heal, thrive, and shine

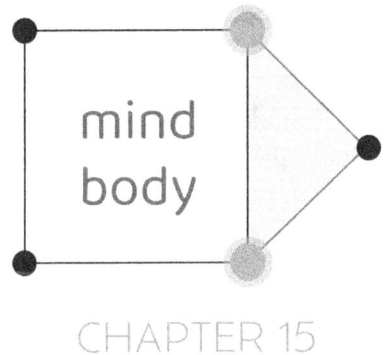

mind
body

Disconnect of Mind and Body

After over two decades of struggling with chronic autoimmune conditions and unresolved neuropathic pain, I was starting to feel the pain diminish and the symptoms reduce in severity. But my condition persisted. I had overhauled my lifestyle— switching to an anti-inflammatory diet, eliminating a large amount of stress in my life, and opting instead to simplify each day, managing how much I took on, distancing myself from people, places, and things that were sapping my energy. I also began to deeply assess my relationship to my body.

Trauma is stored in the body, and so many years of grappling with significant illness conditions had taken its toll. Medical trauma is real! I began to realize there was a disconnect between my mind and body. I noticed that if I experienced a sudden stress from an outside event, that my body would have a stress response like racing heart, gut pain, digestion issues, and neuropathic pain flares from neck down to my fingertips. Attempting to remove the potential triggers from my daily life was not enough to prevent these responses. I noticed that my baseline anxiety level remained rather high regardless of the level of calm in my life.

Our Autonomic Nervous System (ANS) is in our peripheral nervous system and has two subsystems: Sympathetic Nervous System (SNS) and Parasympathetic Nervous System (PNS). The SNS is responsible for the flight-fight response. We share this with all mammals on the planet. When faced with a sudden threat, we instantly choose to flee or fight the threat. But, there are other mobilization states that may be utilized such as freeze or fawn (people pleasing).

When the threat is gone and we perceive we are safe, the SNS damps down and our bodies return to the rest and digest state of the PNS. We see these play out in the wild when a gazelle is chased by a lion. When the gazelle runs to safety and the predator is no longer a threat, the gazelle's body may shake automatically to release the surge of stress from the encounter. Then the gazelle returns to a parasympathetic state and resumes grazing.

In the case of chronic, unrelenting stress, this system can become compromised and the body becomes unable to return to the PNS state. This can happen in health situations like mine, in which one is constantly bombarded with a stress response. Stephen Porges, creator of the Polyvagal Theory, describes three possible states in what he refers to as the Polyvagal Ladder: Relaxed (Ventral Vagal), Mobilized (SNS), and Immobilized (Dorsal Vagal).[1]

The relaxed state is experienced as engaged, hopeful, creative. Here you may be reading a book or painting a picture. The mobilized state is energized and active as a positive state, or stressed and anxious in the negative state. When in positive mobilization, you may be playing a sport, dancing, or performing. When in negative mobilization you are in the flight/fight state. When in the positive immobilized state (hybrid of relaxed and mobilized) you may be dreaming or meditating, or having a bubble bath. The negative immobilization state (hybrid of mobilized and immobilized) may be characterized by depression, hopelessness, worry.

The preliminary solutions I tried—like meditation—did not work well. I felt too wound up, agitated, unable to sit in stillness. At that time, I knew anxiety had claimed center stage in my daily life. I needed something different. Through a friend, I learned of vagus nerve toning, brain retraining, and somatic therapy. The vagus nerve is part of the parasympathetic system. Low vagal tone can be an outcome of chronic stress, trauma, surgery, or disease conditions. It is marked by a lowered ability to regulate emotions. Fortunately, even actions like humming helps tone the vagus nerve.

Brain retraining, from my experience, is essentially about re-teaching your mind that you are safe and there is no threat. This is done through conscious intention to be in the present, practicing breathwork to engage mind and body, and feeling into positive mind states. Finally somatic therapy is focused on working with the body to release trauma. This combination of therapies has been very effective in helping me resolve and reset my nervous system. I still continue these today, and they are my reminder that the mind-body dynamic is essential to well-being.

> *"Your body hears everything your mind says."*
> **—Naomi Judd**

On the Well-being Pyramid, mind and body together affect You as mind-body. Your thoughts are perceived by the mind. Your emotions are experienced in your body. When you consciously connect thoughts and feelings, with an awareness of the link between mental and physical processes, this is a mind-body experience.

What happens when one encounters a disconnect of the integrated system of mind and body?

Disconnect

Most of us have experienced being too "in your head." This may result in cycles of rumination and fatiguing analysis. In those instances, we are detached from the experience of the present. Our thoughts may linger on worries (fear), and regrets, shame or guilt. And that is suffering. Spiritual teacher Ekhart Tolle, urges us to become the watcher of our thoughts, to remember that You are not the mind; you are the watcher of the mind.

If that statement does not make sense to you, you may be completely identified with your thoughts at the moment. Like a cork floating on the ocean's surface, you are tossed about with every new event or occurrence that happens in your life. You get a raise, a new job, or a relationship, and you are happy. You receive a large bill or bad news and suddenly you experience any number of negative emotions—anxiety, worry, or anger. These emotional states likely impact how the rest of your day proceeds.

In this situation, your inner state is completely controlled by outer circumstances. So, with those fears, we grasp at external validators that we are acceptable, safe, winners. How much money, how many material possessions, how many social media likes and followers do you need to finally feel a sense of peace and fulfillment? Also, does it actually work?

The connection between mind and body is evident when your mind identifies a feeling, and your body immediately responds with a physical sensation. A sense of fear or anxiety can feel like a lump in the throat or a flame in your gut.[2] You may feel a fluttery feeling like butterflies in your stomach as a response to excitement. Yet for various reasons, we sometimes repress difficult emotions rather than fully experience them. This may be done unconsciously and as a defense against overwhelming feelings.

Emotions may be repressed for cultural reasons, such as if one's culture, community, or family finds the emotion unacceptable or shameful. The drive for belonging and acceptance may push someone's psyche to bury those feelings from the conscious mind. Other times, feelings are inadvertently repressed because a person was never taught how to acknowledge or manage them. But, repressing feelings is a short-term solution that can lead to long-term issues. Negative emotions you repress from your mind eventually manifest negatively in your body.[3] The body always remembers.

Autoimmune diseases are a class of chronic diseases that are of personal interest to me, as I was diagnosed with autoimmune thyroiditis. It is not yet understood what causes most autoimmune diseases, why a particular disease manifests in one individual, how to reverse the symptoms and impact within the western medicine model, and how to prevent autoimmune disease occurrence in the first place.

Dr. Alan Goldhamer states in the March 7, 2024 podcast of *Heal Thy Self*, that in autoimmune disease, the body's immune system is overly active and attacks its own tissue. Almost like an opposite reaction, in cancer the body's immune system is not "keeping up with aberrant cells through autophagy."[4]

Autoimmune disease is an interesting focal point in considering the inseparable link between mind and body, and the possible repercussions of living a life disconnected from and repressing one's emotions.

Dr. Gabor Mate, a very well-known doctor, author, and speaker, discusses the relationship between stress and disease in his book, *When the Body Says No: Exploring the Stress-Disease Connection*. Referencing autoimmune diseases like rheumatoid disease, multiple sclerosis, and chronic conditions in general, he draws a parallel between the psychological profile of a patient who acquired such illnesses and the disease manifestation itself, likening both to a confusion or "disarray" of boundaries between the self and non-self. For example, this may be a person who does not express healthy anger toward an "attachment figure" but instead directs that anger inward. Similarly, autoimmune disease is one's body turning against itself, with immune cells attacking healthy tissue.[5]

Dr. Mate speaks of the correlation between the repression of emotions and the manifestation of autoimmune and other diseases. He states upon reflection on a patient with scleroderma, that none of her doctors had thought to sit with the patient and have her talk about her life and her feelings. Dr. Mate sat with her and learned a great deal about her life circumstances—child abuse, neglect, instability, and having to "parent" her own siblings from a young age. He learned how she had repressed her own emotions to survive the traumas she experienced. Dr. Mate writes that before modern medicine and medical technology, a doctor had to form a close relationship with the patient, to understand her life and emotional landscape. The doctor relied on a more intuitive assessment of the patient than is sought in modern medicine.

This approach to medicine is making a return through the relatively new medical discipline of psychoneuroimmunology (PNI). PNI addresses the mind and how emotions impact the nervous system and then the immune system. These facets of a human do not exist in isolation with one another. Dr. Mate states that chronic autoimmune disease "involves the entire

PNI super-system, particularly the brain-hormone-immune connections."

Stress significantly affects this system as cortisol production is chronically stimulated, leading to imbalance and dysregulation of the immune system. An immune system gone haywire can cause the body to attack itself, as it occurs in autoimmune disease.

The hypothalamic-pituitary-adrenal (HPA) axis is a key factor in PNI and how it relates to stress disorders. This access and the delicate balance and relationship between its components is key to maintaining a healthy stress response.

When the HPA axis is not functioning properly, an inadequate amount of cortisol is produced, and inflammation manifests. The end result over a period of time could be autoimmune disease. Dr. Dawn-Elise Snipes explains that the HPA axis is the master control center of the stress response, controlling the adrenal glands, gonadal (sex) hormones, cortisol and blood sugar levels, and the immune system.

Dr. Snipes explains that when the brain perceives a potential threat from the sensory data it collects, this triggers the HPA axis. The brain identifies a threat based on prior experiences or the lack of any data about the experience. An array of neurochemicals and blood sugars are released in response to the perceived threat, so that the body is geared up for action. The immune system and sex hormones are suppressed.

In a healthy person, when the perceived stress or danger is no longer present, the HPA and vagus nerve will damp down the stress response and allow one's body to return to its normal state. If the cortisol that should suppress the inflammatory response is unable to do so due to the dysregulation of the HPA, the immune system remains in a heightened state and the body is inflamed. This sets the stage for autoimmune diseases.[6]

Does disease in the body serve a purpose for the patient?

Dr. Mate seems to imply that in his experience working with patients with autoimmune disease, the flare up of the disease often serves to force the patient to do the very actions they spent a lifetime resisting, and learn that those actions would have been the healthy, self-compassionate choice. For example, he noticed that many of his patients could not deny others' requests for their time or energy.[7] This resulted in emotional repression and an inability for an individual to establish healthy boundaries for themselves.

Dr. Mate acknowledges that it is often difficult for a person to accept that their disease may be due to their own life choices and disregarding their true needs. He distinguishes between blame and responsibility.

When we know that we have some agency over the manifestation of disease in the body, and that our own mental stress contributed to the disease, we may be able to change the course of the disease and perhaps reduce symptoms and triggers.

At the core of this is the mind-body as a connected system. Emotions must be consciously acknowledged and expressed. This happens when the mind is in concert with the body. Anyone who has experienced deep grief and succumbed to gut-wrenching sobbing and the aches and pains that accompany it will relate to the mind-body embodiment of sadness. This emotional expression and release generally allows some of the intensity to dissipate, and for the person to feel somewhat better, even amid sadness.

Mark Hyman, a well-known and renowned functional medicine doctor, talks about what a patient can do to improve one's health when facing autoimmune disease in the September 3, 2015 You Tube video, "10 Steps to Reverse Autoimmune Disease." As functional medicine looks for the root cause of disease, so as to heal it at the source, he urges that one must look at the drivers of their autoimmune disease that are causing chronic inflammation. Eliminating the causes is key to reversing the disease condition.

He explains in the video that there are five main causes of autoimmune disease: toxins, microbes, allergens, poor diet, and stress. These triggers interact with a person's body and genetic makeup, disrupting the natural balance needed for optimal health. When harmful influences outweigh positive inputs—such as whole, fresh food, sunlight, clean air and water, restful sleep, physical activity, meaningful connections, and a sense of purpose—the body can become inflamed. This chronic inflammation is a sign of imbalance, reflecting a deeper disconnect between mind and body.[8]

Trauma

Dr. Bessel Van Der Kolk, the trauma authority who wrote *The Body Keeps the Score*, believes trauma is distinct from regular memory, which can fade or be forgotten. "Trauma is a literal inclusion of the past into the present, which can produce physiological effects whether or not the traumatized person consciously remembers the event."[9]

It is the most profound example of mind-body disconnection. Dr. Van Der Kolk explains in his book that disassociation is the core of trauma. The sensory aspects of a traumatic memory infiltrate the present, where they are re-lived over and over by an individual, as if the event is presently occurring. The body's stress hormones are triggered, and they may have rapidly increased heart rate, start breathing faster, or get a migraine. These are all subconscious physical body manifestations of trauma, and the repeated adverse response in the present to the past event is called post-traumatic stress disorder (PTSD).

Dr. Van Der Kolk states that many of his traumatized patients could not feel certain parts of their body. He also writes that our sensory world and our sense of self-awareness are inextricably linked. The key to recovery from trauma therefore, is to "reconnect" mind and body, to re-align the awareness with sensations in the body.

One therapeutic approach to heal trauma is somatic therapy. Three symptom groups of PTSD are intrusions (involuntary and stress-inducing memories of trauma), avoidance (of the trauma-associated stimuli), and persistent physiological hyperarousal. People with PTSD experience a great deal of suffering.[10]

Somatic Experiencing, created by Dr. Peter Levine, focuses on the arousal and training of the nervous system to change the "internal sense of the body." Without it the body will continue to send messages of the past experience to our brain, and the brain interprets these as an impending threat. Dr. Levine explains that a person having a PTSD episode cannot be talked out of it. In those times, the person is stuck in the sympathetic states of flight, fight, or shut down, and the only way to get them out of that state is through bodily movement.[11]

In somatic experiencing, the patient's attention is directed to their internal sensations, instead of the cognitive or emotional aspects of the trauma. By working with the patient in this manner, the patient will gradually decrease their stress response and discover acceptance of their inner sensations and emotion. The goal is to increase a person's interoceptive (internal bodily sensations) and proprioceptive (kinesthetic, body's ability to sense its location, movements, and actions) awareness, so they can "discharge" the trauma.[12]

We learn through considerations of disconnect, dissociation, and trauma, that when the body and mind are not synchronized in communication, we suffer. Our ability to live full, joyous lives is greatly diminished, if not completely halted. The body serves as a gateway to access unresolved emotions. Nurture your own mind-body through practices that foster deep mind-body connection.

Qi Gong, Tai Chi, yoga, and many other movement modalities such as dance enable you to feel mindful joy in movement. For those who are wheel-chair bound or lying in a hospital bed, some of these practices such as Qi Gong are still highly accessible and beneficial. The Feldenkrais Method is a somatic therapy that helps reconnect mind and body to healthy and optimal communication by leveraging the neuroplasticity of the brain.[13]

Chronic pain can create a vicious cycle of more pain when one avoids movement due to fear of more pain. As humans are meant to be mobile and regularly use our bodies throughout the day, avoiding movement due to fear can lead to muscle and joint weakness, which can in turn actually increase one's level of chronic pain. The best approach is to gently ease yourself into movement.

Yoga offers slower-paced variants such as Yin Yoga, in which you can focus on the coordination of breath and gentle movement. Per the U.K.-based Minded Institute, "Brain imaging scans have also associated chronic pain with structural and functional changes in areas such as the prefrontal cortex and hippocampus that indicate the development of anxiety and depression."[14] The mindfulness associated with practising yoga can counter these mental states. I have tried many types of exercises and movement over the years, in an effort to either work with or ignore chronic pain. I always return to yoga as an accessible modality that supports my mind and body. Every asana, or yoga posture I attempt is a reminder to myself that

I am still alive, I am here, and I am meant to thrive despite the pain.

CHAPTER 15 REFLECTIONS

A very common vicious cycle involves inadequate sleep and excess caffeine to 'boost' one's weary mind and body. Whether it's teens in high school (a crucial time when sleep is essential to growth), or it's the working adult juggling long hours, family demands, and social engagements–if ever there is a perfect example of overriding the body's signals of fatigue or pain, this is it. Unfortunately caffeine is not energy. It simply delivers a short-lived and false sense of focus and energy. In reality, caffeine also increases adrenaline and cortisol, and it can disrupt sleep patterns. You may experience jitters in your body. Both caffeine and lack of adequate sleep can disrupt the mind-body relationship, and leave you less able to cope with daily stress and change.

1. Reflect on a time when you felt too much in your head. What were your thoughts at that time? What emotions were you experiencing?

2. What was an instance when you overroad or ignored messages from your body? What were your thoughts and what bodily sensation did you choose to ignore? What consequences did you experience as a result?

3. What mind-body practice do you do? What is beneficial to you about this practice? If you do not do any, consider implementing one for a few weeks, noting any benefits to your mind, body, and well-being

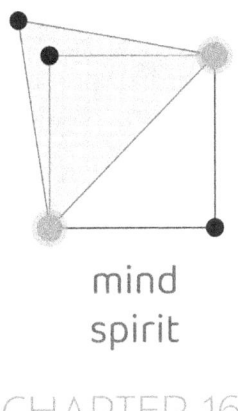

mind
spirit

The Heart of the Mind

One of the biggest lessons I have learned through my journey with chronic illness, pain, and disability is realizing the importance of my intuition and its connection to creativity. Over twenty years ago, when I was hit with debilitating symptoms and Western medicine did not have a diagnosis for me, I felt quite abandoned. There was no external resource or support system that helped me navigate this unknown world of illness. There was no concrete information onto which my mind could cling for certainty. I lived in a great deal of fear for many years, trying to keep my mind distracted from what I saw as a bleak reality with no end in sight.

After yet another round of meetings with medical specialists who could only offer me a blank stare as to what might be next for me, I suddenly realized that none of them had the answers. Not one of them had any idea of how to help. I had fallen through the cracks of the medical system, and I continued to feel unwell and in pain. It was then that my spirit, my heart, made its presence loudly known. I understood intuitively that Western doctors would not be the ones to help me heal. I wanted to heal and reverse my conditions, and for that, I would have to look elsewhere.

The epiphany from my spirit, which had held safe my hope all this time, was that I must look into alternative modalities. And so began what has now been a four-year journey through holistic terrain, engaging functional practitioners and doctors, herbalists, naturopathic specialists, and Eastern medicine doctors of TCM and Ayurveda. I learned so much about the agency I do have to create the health I wish to have.

This decision to investigate a holistic healing path symbolized a shift in energy from mind to heart. Whereas I had only trusted my mind to logically analyze, research, and determine my decisions based on the recommendations from the disease-diagnosis model of Western care, now I gave space and considered the advice from my heart. My intuition had a clear message—there was another way. My spirit and intuition illuminated the lifestyle changes I would have to make, should I want to heal myself.

I never fully abandoned Western medicine, nor the recommendations from allopathic doctors. Western medicine remains outstanding and excels in so many areas, especially in situations in which surgery is required and in pinpointing drug therapies for specific diseases. However, I now weigh the possibilities and determine in every scenario what would best serve my healing.

My shift in perspective naturally led me to reconsider the very nature of healing itself—-to rethink the heart, and how we have defined it. Although the heart is a part of the body, yet we often refer to it as that which is not mind or body, but of what I have defined as spirit in this book. In Buddhist philosophy, the heart and mind are one. The word *citta* in Sanskrit means heart-mind. Buddhist monk and teacher Jack Kornfield explains that citta is "all our thoughts, our feelings and emotions, responses, intuition, temperament, and consciousness itself."[1] So citta is essentially consciousness. The actions that are inspired through the heart-mind are those that will demonstrate a higher consciousness. Heart and mind working together synergistically can provide us with the heart-centered global thinking that sees all of humanity as a family worthy of altruism and hope.

Humans often go wrong in handling their minds and hearts. When people experience difficult moments, perhaps a painful breakup of a relationship, or the death of a loved one, they may put up "walls" to guard their heart. Any barrier between mind and heart serves to disconnect the mind-spirit and will affect all facets of your life, beyond the relationship fallout or grief with which one may be dealing.

Intuition, per the Merriam-Webster dictionary, is "the power or faculty of attaining to direct knowledge or cognition without evident rational thought and inference." Intuition, also referred to as gut feeling, is the felt sense of awareness of a thought, and that the thought is right for us. We use intuition most often when making abstract choices, such as whether a person has good or ill intent.

Intuition acts on instinct as opposed to analytic thinking. In an August 22, 2023 article in Psychology Today titled *Intuition: What It Is and How It Works?*, Dr. Thomas R. Verny writes of an experiment conducted by the HeartMath Institute, a non-profit that conducts research on well-being, stress reduction, and peace, which demonstrated that when human subjects were presented with a series of emotional pictures, the heart received and responded to the emotional quality of the content before the brain.[2]

According to the study, the information was received in the following order: heart, brain, gut. The vagus nerve is the longest cranial nerve, and passes from head to neck, to thorax and abdomen. This nerve connects brain and gut and brain and heart as part of the gut-brain and heart-brain axes.[3]

We have in our gut the enteric nervous system, which contains about one hundred million neurons.[4] The gut transmits sensations to the brain which can sense this information through interoception, the brain's ability to sense the body's internal state. Most of this occurs unconsciously. The signals that are transmitted to our conscious awareness in the brain are our gut feelings, or intuition.

Human intuition is itself a complex phenomenon, involving long-term memory, contextual understanding, emotional investment, and tapping into feelings. Joel Pearson, neuroscientist and author of *The Intuition Toolkit* explains intuition as unconscious information that the conscious mind utilizes for better decision-making. He explains that the body registers information and the subconscious can tap into the body's cues in guiding intuition.[5]

Gut feelings have been a key part of humans' survival instincts since the beginning of humanity. At times, the intuition may be incorrect. Perhaps this may be because we have misinterpreted a fear-based decision as an intuitive one; biases or misinformation may also muddy the intuitive channel. Pearson refers to these as "misintuition".

How does the heart or spirit influence intuition and creativity? When we use the expression "follow your heart," we imply that the heart knows better than the thinking mind in those instances. We acknowledge that the heart has wisdom and can serve as a superior guide in making important life decisions.

According to the HeartMath Institute (heartmath.org), becoming heart coherent means one is fully aligned in mind, body, spirit, and emotions. Deborh Rozman of the HeartMath Institute explains that the heart has its own nervous system and sensory neurons that process information independent of the mind.[6] They have found that a specific rhythmic pattern of a heart in coherence will enable a person to have a greater ability for intuitive discernment. In this state of coherence, the sympathetic and parasympathetic nervous systems are working together in harmony.

The intuitive abilities of the heart were quantified and studied by the Institute with an experiment that measures heart rate variability (HRV). HRV measures the time in between heart beats. This time fluctuates continuously, depending on what you are doing and feeling. The variability is a measure of the adaptability of your heart. A low HRV can be indicative of current and future health issues. It correlates with how well you manage stressful events.[7] What is the relationship between HRV and your brain?

According to a March 1, 2023 article in Frontiers in Neuroscience, "*The connection between heart rate variability (HRV), neurological health, and cognition: A literature review,*" HRV is managed by the Central Autonomic Network (CAN).[8] This includes your brain, spinal cord, and peripheral nervous system. The CAN regulates involuntary fundamental processes like blood pressure, heart rate, respiration, and digestion. Based on feedback from the heart producing low HRV, your brain reads the lack of coherence as stress or threat, two mind states that are not conducive to creative or intuitive thinking.[8]

Practicing the emotional states of compassion, kindness, and gratitude has a positive effect on heart coherence, just as states of stress, worry, and fear shift you out of it. Practices like meditation and mindfulness help move mind and heart to a higher state of alignment and attunement within oneself, others, and the world around them. As the heart represents our intuitive intelligence and spirit, it makes sense that we utilize both the mind and the spirit in making important decisions and navigating life.

This mind-spirit coherence has tremendous benefits to not only the individual, but to others around them. The HeartMath institute refers to this as social coherence. It states that the electromagnetic energy of an individual's heart rhythm is being transmitted out into the world, up to five feet away. Heartmath measures this energy using an electrocardiogram (ECG) and renders it visible as waves recorded on thermal paper.

The institute has done experiments that prove one individual's heart coherence and radiating feelings of love and compassion are received by and positively influence others in proximity. From this standpoint, the interconnectedness we have with each other and other living beings cannot be denied. Per the HeartMath Institute, we are all affecting a planetary "global information field." One person's mind-spirit well-being does indeed impact all of us! In the next chapter we will discuss the next dual dynamic on the Well-being Pyramid—mind-space.

CHAPTER 16 REFLECTIONS

Consider an instance when you suddenly felt a hunch, or a "knowing" about something. Nothing in your environment is stating that message to you, yet your mind has picked it up and you feel it in your body to be true. What environment were you in when this occurred? Did you feel relaxed and centered within yourself? Being in nature, listening to music, or journaling can be moments that encourage these intuitive hits.

1. How in tune are you with your intuition? What is a circumstance or decision for which you exercised your intuitive muscle? What was the resulting outcome?

2. Optional exercise: Choose one tracker device that measures HRV (Heartmath's Inner Balance device, Oura ring, Whoop). For one week, track and record your HRV at the same time daily upon awakening but before getting out of bed. Also track daily your lifestyle factors that could impact HRV including the duration and intensity of exercise, alcohol consumption, stress level, processed food consumption. How consistent is your HRV from day to day? What lifestyle choices improve your HRV (higher score) and what worsens HRV (lower score)?

3. Practice heart-centered breathing meditation for five minutes: Place hands on heart and breathe in for a count of six and out for a count of six and repeat. While breathing, visualize the breath going in and out from your heart. Note sensations, mind state, mood upon completion

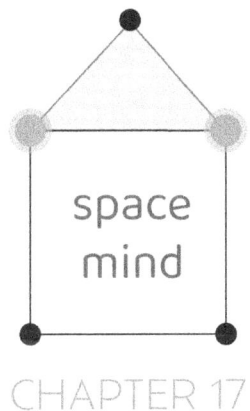

space
mind

The Mind's Perception of Space and Time

The traditional walkabout, undertaken by young Aboriginal men as a rite of passage, has a deeply spiritual origin. As a challenging rite of passage for an Aboriginal youth, it requires the use of a keen and centered mind to traverse the harsh ancestral Australian outback terrain and successfully use the environment's available resources to survive. Prior to the undertaking, the young man is taught through song, dance, and oral stories. He is instructed on how to survive the terrain on his own, taking advantage of the environment to provide for his basic needs of food, water, and shelter. It is a test of mental fortitude and bravery, as well as a relationship with the environment in which it is all too apparent that humans are only one of many creatures surviving in it. Here the dynamic relationship between mind and space (environment) is transformative for those who engage in the perilous journey.

Mind, Space, and SpaceTime

Since the beginning of time humans have been engaging with nature, either living harmoniously with it, seeking to "tame" it or very often strip it of resources. The former fosters reverence, love, and a sense of unity with one's environment, and the latter can be seen as a fear-based, disconnected reaction to something that is inevitably more powerful than any single human life. But true well-being is not found in domination or detachment; rather, it arises from a conscious, reciprocal relationship with our surroundings. Cultivating a deep and mindful connection between your inner world and the space you inhabit is fundamental to this harmony.

The mind and space dimensions have been discussed separately in previous chapters, but how do they synergistically impact your well-being? To explore this, we must first understand why humans have established concepts such as space and time to understand their environment. Our experience of reality is deeply tied to these constructs, influencing how we perceive and interact with the world.

Traditionally, we view time and space as distinct, but Einstein's theory of relativity introduced the idea of spacetime—a four-dimensional continuum of length, width, depth, and time. In this framework, events are not just defined by their location in space but also by their position in time and space. Our perception of events, shaped by our mindset, beliefs, and focus, determines how we experience reality. In other words, our outlook on life influences not just our internal state but also how we engage with external circumstances.

This idea aligns with philosophical perspectives like nonduality, which suggests that everything is interconnected—one unified existence rather than separate entities. Rupert Spira, an author, speaker, and teacher of nonduality, explains that we humans created the concept of time as a "container" for all forgotten past events and experiences, and that each of our memories creates time.[1] He surmises that universal consciousness goes through a similar process of forgetting objects. Space is the "container" that houses these objects. Each human consciousness is a localized, minute aspect of universal consciousness that can only simultaneously experience a few objects at a given time. Thus, per Spira, your mind as a single consciousness creates the space to house all forgotten objects. Just as time does not actually exist, neither does space.[1]

These are rather esoteric explanations for the human constructs of time and space, and we tend to take them for granted—afterall, time and space is measurable in our three-dimensional world. Indian mystic Sadhguru, states that time and space have been created because of the physicality of the human experience, i.e., because we each have a body, time and space exists. So, the mind creates both concepts to make sense of and organize its earthly experience.

It is rather difficult to conclude that space does not really exist when we experience it as reality. We can move our bodies through space, we can interact with objects in space. We can believe our own illusions about space.

These illusions are illustrated in the pages of comic books in which the body of a character in a frame is foreshortened using a three-point perspective to create a dynamic superhero pose. Comic artists achieve extraordinary depth in one frame using this technique, yet, our eyes send signals to our brains, and we believe the illusion. Does this mean the space within a comic book frame is not "real"?

Illusions of space occur in still life works of art that create a sense of depth with paint on a two-dimensional canvas. We see Claude Monet's *Water Lily Pond* and instantly believe in the scene it is depicting. We feel we can see across the pond. Even Salvador Dali's surrealist paintings that seek to play with and distort perspective still achieve a sense of depth. Dali sought to challenge the viewer's expectations of the reality of space in his painting *The Persistence of Memory*.[2]

He depicts a familiar landscape in the background which is in stark contrast to the soft, melting watches, ants crawling all over a pocket watch, and his own unusual and amorphous self-portrayal in the foreground. It is the intended visual confusion that Dali sought to capture that draws the eye to the painting, while incorporating landscape, still-life, and self-portrait in a single work.

Dali was conveying through the symbolism of this painting the passage of time, timelessness, and his belief that past, present, and future are subjective. The illusions of space we create are very real to us within the context of the mediums with which they are created and the three-dimensional perspective they achieve. It is all just space and the willingness of our minds to believe it.

I love a movie that draws me in and immerses me in the storytelling. While fully engaged in watching a movie, I have no awareness of actual time or space. I *am* the characters, and if it is well done, I feel their feelings and live their lives. I love epic stories, fantasy, science fiction, action and adventure, romance, and comedy. I'll watch anything but horror because I feel my nervous system simply does not need that type of agitation!

Movies such as *Avatar* stay with me forever. The fact that we buy into and fully accept the phenomenal world-building of a movie is testimony to the human mind's capacity to rationalize that the created space is plausible and congruent with what we know space to be. Within that space, we may rage, laugh, cry, and even feel transformed. The experience is real, and so is the impact on our emotional state and well-being.

We are well into the artificial intelligence age, and AI innovations are rapidly progressing. Generative AI systems like ChatGPT currently produce written and visual content. Other generative AI tools like Dall-E 3, Midjourney, or Leonardo can be used to create visual art. It is logical to assume that entire virtual worlds will be AI generated in the near future. Games like Fortnite already do this. Virtual concerts have been created. But, in terms of having a unified immersive metaverse space for all humans in which we can work, meet, and socialize, we are not there yet.

Also, who knows if humans will want to live in virtual lives for extended periods of time while their physical body languishes in a chair at home and apart from the natural world. The human body is meant to be in motion. We are already seeing the health impacts of sedentary jobs and how "sitting is the new smoking." True, we may be engaging in that virtual experience by moving on a 360 degree treadmill that allows for motion in any direction, but will it be the same as the sensual experience of engaging with our natural spaces in real life?

We can't effectively escape from our inextricable ties to the natural world and our connection and dependence on the earth for life as material beings. It will be interesting to see how the metaverse story unfolds in the future. Regardless, if we are embodied in an avatar that is moving through the virtual world and interacting with others and the objects of that world, that space will be as real to our minds as is our physical world. Such is the adaptability of the human mind and its need to define and understand space.

Theoretical physicists like Michio Kaku speak of string theory, a subset of particle physics which incorporates quantum physics and the theory of relativity. Whereas our three-dimensional space and the fourth dimension of time is what we experience, string theory postulates that there are ten "spacetime" dimensions.[3] The additional six spatial dimensions are potentially tightly curled through a process known as compactification.[4] They are not discernible in our three-dimensional space.

Physicists like Albert Einstein and Stephen Hawking strove to explain how our universe works by finding The Theory of Everything.[5] They struggled with the question, "Is there one equation that incorporates both quantum physics and Einstein's general relativity?" The theories that explain the quantum world do not seem to apply to the large-scale universe and gravitational forces. Many different string theories were developed. From this arose M-theory, which unifies all the string theories.[6]

In terms of defining space in higher dimensions, the hypercube or tesseract represents a four-dimensional object. In the fifth dimension, the idea of parallel universes exists, as a fifth-dimensional being can be in more than one location at once. Potentially other versions of yourself exist and could be living very different lives! In the sixth dimension, a being can see all timelines (past, present, future) of all versions of themselves. The theories on higher dimensions get even more mind boggling as you contemplate the complexity of each higher dimension.

Why is this even important in a book about authentic well-being? First, we make many assumptions with our minds about what space really is, as we only live in a 3D world. We understand that we affect and are affected by everything else in our world. This impacts our overall well-being. If what our minds know as space is actually much more complex and nuanced than it appears, it stands to reason that there is so much more that could impact our well-being but is not knowable with humanity's current level of understanding and consciousness. What more can we realize about our existence and ourselves if we can truly perceive quantum reality?

We are shaped by how our minds perceive and connect to space, and how our defined spaces influence us. I liken it to the light we can see. The light spectrum visible to the human eye is delineated by seven colors—red, orange, yellow, green, blue, indigo, and violet. What if we could comprehend and understand a thousand more colors? Would we not want to experience that breathtaking beauty? It's only speculation, but I think that redefining our concept of space could have a far greater impact on our sense of wellness, and possibly lead to a much greater understanding of our consciousness. In the next chapter we will explore the relationship dynamic of body-spirit and how it impacts well-being.

CHAPTER 17 REFLECTIONS

The Afro-futuristic world depicted in the *Wakanda* movies is a beautiful depiction of a technologically-advanced and highly socially cooperative civilization. It's interesting to consider each of their sources of power and what energizes their world. In the *Wakanda* movies, the central source of power which serves as the energy generator for all their advanced technology is vibranium. Vibranium, derived from a meteor, has limitless capabilities. In the *Star Wars* franchise, the source of power is the Force. In *Harry Potter*, the power source was magic. In *The Lord of the Rings*, the Rings of Power are the ultimate sources. In all these examples, the characters must connect with the power source to harness it for their purposes. The source is bigger than any one individual, pervades their worlds, and connects all living beings. Each characters' relationship to their environment is at its core about their relationship to the source of power. In that context, the world of the *Na'vi* in the movie *Avatar* is about the deep interconnectedness of all living beings to each other and the natural environment.

1. What is your relationship to the environments in which you interact? In what environment do you feel the most centered and well? How does that space support you?

2. If you were to engage in a world-building exercise and create any environment you wish (fantastical elements are encouraged), describe what that would be. How

would you engage with that world? How would it enhance your well-being?

3. Reflect on a time when you felt confined in a particular space, inside or outside. What steps did you take to change your relationship to that space?

4. Reflect on a time when you felt unity with a space, when you temporarily ceased to be self-conscious

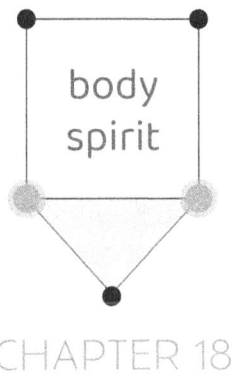

Accessing Spirit through the Body

On my birthday a decade ago, I had just suited up with a jumpsuit and gear. I stood next to my friends, waiting to have my harness and gear checked by the instructor. We had received detailed instruction on the whole end-to-end process, and I was excited about this skydiving adventure. Details about the experience, like the height of the skydive escape me now—maybe about 10,000 feet. We boarded a small plane in the order and arrangement stipulated by the guides. It was a tandem jump, so I felt I was in good hands with the certified instructor. Once we reached the optimal altitude, it was go time!

The exhilaration of standing at the open door and staring at nothing but sky made my breath catch in my throat. My whole body felt electric and alive and there was no thought, no rumination. Just present moment awareness tinged with fear (excitement?). While jumping and hurtling through space in freefall, other than the momentary thought, "I hope I can breathe", my mind was still and keenly aware. The freefall was rather quick in retrospect. Before I knew it, the chute was opened and I was lifted up in a sudden *woosh* as the parachute filled with air. From there everything slowed down and I was a bird, gliding on the wind, and perusing the world below as I dangled from my harness and the parachute slowly lowered toward the ground. My feet touched first and I sat down, feeling awe and wonder that it was even possible to have this experience.

Why did I want to skydive? To challenge myself and get out of my comfort zone, to feel alive, to remind myself that life is about taking chances. All that was true, but even more so for me, it was to choose aliveness and expansion over the fear and contraction that often accompanies complex chronic illness. My momentum through space and gravity was a temporary letting go of the density of the body to feel the lightness of the spirit. Dancing elicits a similar feeling.

"Stop acting so small. You are the universe in ecstatic motion." —**Rumi**

Ritual dance has long been considered a means to connect with spirit and to access the divine. The Hindu God Shiva is known as Lord of Dance and the Cosmic Dancer depicted in sculpture as Nataraja. The Nataraja represents Shiva as creator, preserver, and destroyer, and the infinite cycle of time. Here, Shiva is encircled by a ring that represents the cosmos. Shiva as the cosmic dancer symbolizes all life and its deep connection to the divine.[1]

The Nataraja is shown as both male and female, therefore neither male nor female. The dance of life and connection to spirit transcends earthly identifications of the body and a binary identification of the physical form. Thus, the spirit accesses the divine through the body and movement with a desire to reach beyond earthly limitations and engage with the higher Self, universal consciousness, the Divine, or God, whichever word holds meaning to you.

The whirling dervishes of Sufi mysticism, a mystical sect of Islam, exemplify the desire to connect spirit with the divine through movement of the body.[2] Rumi, the ancient Persian poet and philosopher, explained that the whirling of the body on one's own axis allows the spirit to be set free from the body to commune with the divine. The dervishes wear white as a symbol of faith and purity.

Dance is deeply spiritual for the people of the African continent. For traditional Africans, the body and its expressions are divine.[3] The goal is often physical exertion to achieve oneness with the Creator, or God. Their styles of dance are as varied as the continent itself, home to thousands of tribes and cultures. Some ritual dances have a goal for the dancer to reach an ecstatic trance which signifies communion with the Divine. All ritual dances incorporate spirit, which can mean the spirits of plants, animals, ancestors, or deities.

There are many other rich cultural examples of the spiritual role of dance for various religions and ethnic communities. Dance has always been a part of human spiritual expression and will continue to be revered for the preservation and legacy of these traditions. For so many around the world, dance is the opportunity to both "honor the supernatural powers and to unite with such a supernatural power" in the blending of the fundamental human dynamics of body and spirit.[4]

This deep connection between movement and spirituality suggests that dance is more than just physical expression—it is an energetic practice, a way of channeling and harmonizing unseen forces. In many traditions, dance is believed to awaken and align the body's subtle energies, reinforcing the idea that human beings are not just physical entities but also energetic ones. People who are very five-senses oriented, or materialists, may have trouble believing in humans as purely energetic beings. Yet each of us has a subtle energy body, also referred to as the human biofield or energy field.

I find it fascinating that western medicine, although focused on the physical body and its biochemical processes, utilizes energy medicine in diagnosis and treatment. Technologies that make use of energy, such as Magnetic Resonance Imaging (MRI), electrocardiogram (EKG) ultrasounds, electroencephalogram (EEG), and Computerized Tomography (CT or CAT) Scan have long been a part of standard care. For example, MRIs utilize magnets and sonic energy to produce images. We accept that the biochemistry of a human can respond to a magnetic field and radio waves by aligning the hydrogen protons within the body. By introducing radio waves and altering the magnetic field, a series of cross-sectional images are produced. Ultrasound units emit sound waves, then capture and read the echoes that are reflected from the tissues or organs being imaged. This is measurable energy emanating from the body.[5]

Western allopathic medicine has historically distanced itself from anything it deemed as alternative practices. Now modalities like Reiki, acupuncture, and acupressure are widely accepted and categorized as "complementary and alternative" (CAM) to western medicine practices. Some hospitals offer these therapies as adjunct to the regular allopathic care.

When eastern and alternative energy medicine therapeutic practices are fully researched through evidence-based studies, incorporated into the Western medicine paradigm, and are a standard part of healing through energy medicine, we may be able to improve health outcomes at an astounding rate.

Western and Eastern healing practices have fundamentally different approaches. Western medicine looks for symptoms, strives to produce a diagnosis, and focuses on individual organs or organ systems. Eastern practices, as well as ancient Shamanic and indigenous healing from around the world, see the person as a whole being. Treatments are used to remedy the whole person. The disciplines of Reiki, Traditional Chinese Medicine, acupuncture, Ayurveda, yoga, pranic healing, laying hands (healing touch), quantum healing, and plant medicine, are some examples of ancient tools that include healing via the body's subtle energy systems.

Energy medicine involves two types of energy, measurable and immeasurable. Measurable energy includes waves of sound, light, and electromagnetism. The thus far immeasurable or putative energy is the human electromagnetic field. This is *prana* in Ayurveda, ancient Indian system of medicine. It is *chi* or *qi* in Traditional Chinese Medicine. In both ancient Eastern systems, the energy is described as running along pathways through the body. Donna Eden, founder of the Eden Energy Medicine system which strives to bridge between biological systems and subtle energy systems, focuses on healing illness through harmonizing the body's energies.[6] Since the subtle energies reflect the state of health of the person, managing these subtle energies is the key to your health and vitality. How might we do this ourselves? One such therapeutic modality is tai chi.

Developed in China in the 12th century A.D., tai chi combines gentle movement, balance, breathing, with cognitive and mental health benefits on memory, stress, sleep, and mood.[7] A while ago, I learned tai chi in a group class. At this time, I was having a great deal of trouble relaxing or sitting in stillness due to a dysregulated nervous system that was borne from having struggled for years with the complexity of a chronic illness. I was very appreciative of tai chi as a type of moving meditation. It requires my entire focus to remember the movement sequences, orient my body to balance, and coordinate both the hand movements and placement as well as the specific footwork. I highly encourage anyone to learn this beautiful modality that energizes the body, deeply engages the mind, and enlivens the spirit.

CHAPTER 18 REFLECTIONS

We are here in physical form, inhabiting a physical space. The requirement is that we move frequently and ideally in harmony with ourselves and our environment. We are energy in motion. It can be a spiritual practice, such as walking meditation. This enhances mindfulness and well-being as we remain present and aware of our bodies and the environment around us.

1. What was an experience you had during which you moved your body in a way that was so freeing you felt a closeness to your spirit? What were the sensations, thoughts, and emotions experienced?

2. What is something new you would like to try to connect with the body-spirit dynamic? What about this is appealing to you?

3. Reflect on your thoughts about energy healing modalities, such as those mentioned in this chapter. What has been most beneficial for you and what outcome made it so helpful? If you haven't tried any energy healing modalities, what would you be willing to try?

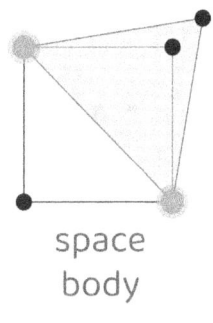

space
body

Choreography of Body and Space

According to the World Freerunning Parkour Federation parkour is "the act of moving from point "a" to point "b" using the obstacles in your path to increase your efficiency". It originated as training in the French Special Forces.[1] Parkour develops confidence, physical strength,and problem-solving skills. It also helps build confidence and self-esteem, and is especially beneficial for kids to learn. All that and more is achieved by changing the relationship of your body's movement through space. This relationship of body and space is fundamental to each of us.

We are physically embodied entities in a physical environment. We first begin to understand our world by our experiential engagement with it. One of the first discoveries infants make is the boundary between Self and Non-Self. My earliest memory was as an infant lying in a crib and staring at my hand as I turned it around and around. Although I have no recollection of the thoughts in my mind at that time, I think I was fascinated by this extremity of mine—an object in space—that I could move at will. Thus began my journey toward self-awareness. The journal article in The journal article in *Child Development* describes this as "visual-kinesthetic matching." (Brownell et al., 2007). This is the foundation from which develops objective self-awareness (oneself as an object of perception), and later reflective self-awareness (mirror self-recognition) at the age of twenty-four to twenty-six months.[2]

Not only do we establish the boundary between self and non-self, but as we grow and are influenced by factors outside ourselves, we establish the acceptable space between the boundary of our body and other people's bodies. This varies by relationship type, and if the boundaries you have understood as acceptable are violated it can be exceedingly difficult to manage and will have an adverse impact on well-being.

Humans establish social rules for navigating shared space and engaging with others. Personal space is "the distance from another person at which one feels comfortable when talking to or being next to that other person," according to Merriam-Webster. This distance is subjective and influenced by factors such as culture, status, gender, relationship, and personality.

These distinctions help establish social norms around personal space and ownership. During the height of the COVID-19 pandemic, social distancing disrupted human connection, leading to emotional distress for many longing for simple gestures of connection—handshakes, hugs, and shared meals.

Beyond personal space, our relationship with the physical environment also shapes our interactions and experiences. When we move through space, we are in relationship to the space. In a ballroom, dancers share an unspoken agreement on how to navigate the space harmoniously. Typically, each couple has a shared silent understanding about their proximity to each other and to the other ballroom couples. Music acts as a catalyst, synchronizing movement and fostering a shared experience.

Dance is one of the most joyous integrations of body and space exhilarating both the dancer and the audience.. The dancer feels the effects of the released endorphins, as the brain's reward center is set in motion. Dance is extremely beneficial for the body, helping to improve coordination, strength, flexibility, muscle tone, and cardiovascular health.

For millennia, dance has been a fundamental part of human culture, serving both social and spiritual roles. Dance benefits the observer as well, promoting relaxation and reducing anxiety.[3] When you are watching a dancer and visualizing yourself doing the dance, the same parts of your brain as the dancer's light up! This is referred to as functional equivalence—a mental "rehearsal". The more senses you involve in this process, the more beneficial the experience. The music that accompanies dance is a key part of this engagement for all parties involved.

Dance promotes neurological health, engaging the nervous system in ways that enhance movement and cognition. Researchers are exploring dance therapy as a treatment for Parkinson's disease, a neurodegenerative disorder that impairs movement. Programs like the one at Stanford utilize dance therapy to improve Parkinson's patients' motor and cognitive functions.[4] Other diseases that impair the central nervous system, including multiple sclerosis and Alzheimer's have been shown to benefit as well from this method of treatment.[5]

Play music for a toddler and watch as they begin to move and respond to the rhythm. According to The Greater Good Magazine, this instinct is hardwired within us and is evident by three weeks of age![6] The body's movement through the space it occupies is called locomotor movement. When we move in response to music, our entire body benefits. This highlights the complex relationship our bodies have with space. We are constantly gathering input from the environment through our senses. Through our bodies we continually change and adapt how we move based on that information.

Earth is the space on which each of us dwells. Our physical vitality and ability to thrive is tied to the planet. We are in constant relationship with the earth and the more directly connected we are, the greater our well-being. What does it mean to be connected to the earth? Natural plant substances we ingest are one of the fundamental examples of this connection's impact.

Since the dawn of human existence, we have studied the flora around us. By trial, error, and centuries of observation, we have discovered plants and herbs that sustain, elevate, and heal us. Those discoveries have become collective knowledge passed down through generations. In every part of the world, herbalism has evolved from ancient origins. Even for many indigenous populations today, herbal medicine is a central part of their healing practices. Herbalism is practiced worldwide in various forms, including Indian Ayurvedic medicine, Traditional Chinese Medicine, Traditional African Medicine, Native American Medicine, Iranian Islamic Medicine, and South American Medicine.[7]

It is remarkable that we have pinpointed specific herbs that can be dried, distilled, infused, decocted, or made into tinctures, all with consistent and beneficial results. That underscores the profound therapeutic relationship between our health and the planet. Knowing that there are herbs that can support well-being with potentially less side effects fosters a greater sense of autonomy over one's health. There is solace in knowing that the planet provides us with the solutions for healing.

One must note that herbs are medicinal and can interact with drugs. It is essential to work with a herbal expert who understands these interactions. Many pharmaceuticals in Western medicine are derived from plants. For example, aspirin was sourced from willow bark, with salicylic acid being the key ingredient. Today, a synthetic version is used in aspirin. What a benefit it would be if herbal knowledge and usage were woven into allopathic medicine! This can happen if Western medicine adopts a truly integrative approach, incorporating herbal treatments alongside conventional care.

Triphala, a polyherb in Ayurvedic medicine, is a blend of three fruits: Amala or Indian gooseberry, Bibhitaki, and Haritaki. I recently had to undergo an outpatient surgical procedure, followed by a week of antibiotics. As a result, I experienced disrupted digestion and gut pain. Triphala helped to mitigate the symptoms by reducing inflammation and aiding in digestion. It allowed me to get the much needed full night of sleep, instead of waking up in the middle of the night with abdominal pain. It's astounding that this blend was developed thousands of years ago and understood to work synergistically together–and the source is fruit!

The dual dynamic of body and space illustrates how connected we are through our physical form to the earth that supports us. We are connected to it in spirit as well. In the next chapter, we will cover the final dual dynamic of spirit-space.

CHAPTER 19 REFLECTIONS

In the modern western world, we habitually seek out pills or supplements to support our health, or in the hope that these synthetically-derived medications will help us heal. Sometimes there are medications that truly benefit us in specific circumstances. For instance, if you develop an itchy rash from skin contact with something that your body assesses as a threat, application of hydrocortisone will instantly provide relief. Or, if you have bloating and indigestion from a heavy meal, a dose of antacids may quickly mitigate the symptoms. Our modern world's "pill for an ill" approach has indeed made us less connected to direct solutions from our environment—solutions with much less cost. If you break off the tip of an aloe plant and apply the salve to a rash, it will provide soothing relief. Ginger, with its anti-nausea and anti-inflammatory properties is fantastic for digestion relief. In Ayurveda, CCF tea is a staple for indigestion. It is composed of equal parts of cumin, coriander, and fennel seeds which are steeped in hot water to make a tea. Our external world can provide us with non-habit forming solutions without side effects. This is the deep connection between the earth and the health of our bodies.

1. When do you feel the most connected with your body and space? Describe the sensations

2. What is an example of a time when space presented physical obstacles that required you to change how you move your body to overcome it, e.g., a wall, or

tree branches covering a path on a hike? What sensory inputs did you utilize to move through the space? Note your body awareness, balance, how you regulate your muscle force, or visually perceive depth.

3. Play a favorite song and dance to it, putting all your attention on the sensations of your body as it moves through space. Note the effects on mood and stress

spirit
space

CHAPTER 20

Qualia and Consciousness

Maharishi Mahesh Yogi was the creator of Transcendental Meditation (TM). Millions around the world practice this type of meditation technique, and numerous studies have proven its benefits to the individual. The Maharishi Effect, a phenomenon first reported in a 1976 research paper, suggests that if 1 percent of a population practiced the TM program, the quality of life of that whole population would improve. One study reported that the crime rate decreased by 16 percent. A 1987 statistical analysis documented a decrease in the crime rate of Washington D.C., Metro Manila, and the Union Territory of Delhi.[1] These findings suggest a profound link between collective meditation, consciousness, and societal well-being, and is an extraordinary testament to the ability of spirit to effect change through space. It is also evidence of our connection to each other as a felt experience through consciousness.

Consciousness is at the core of all experience. It is identified through the experiencer, shaping our perception of reality. There is a word that represents the experiential and sensory nature of consciousness, and that is *qualia*. I searched for a simple, straightforward explanation of qualia and was hard-pressed to find one. One definition is that qualia is the "intrinsic quality of conscious experience." Defining qualia is like defining consciousness itself—an elusive yet fundamental aspect of our experience. Looking at a red rose, your internal experience of red is qualia. There are no physical properties that can be used by way of explanation. It is simply the subjective sensory experience. Listening to the sound of a waterfall elicits an internal experience of qualia derived from the sights, sounds, and even smell that cannot be put into words.

Does qualia exist beyond human experience? Can plants and trees, lacking brains and nervous systems, still possess a form of consciousness? It is simple to dismiss the question with a resounding "No!" Yet, certain plant behaviors challenge this assumption, raising intriguing questions about their ability to perceive and respond to stimuli. Trees and plants do not possess the anatomy to be conscious. They have no brain, central nervous system, cognition, or awareness. What evidence if any has been collected on plant consciousness?

As a child in Delhi, I was fascinated by a potted plant in my grandparents' yard: *Mimosa pudica*, or the touch-me-not plant.

When I touched its leaves, they would fold in immediately as a defense mechanism. This plant's leaf movement intrigued scientists, leading to an experiment exploring plant memory. That behavior alone does not provide sufficient evidence for plant consciousness. However, an article in the *National Geographic* reports on an experiment done using the mimosa pudica that entailed a steel rail and platform on which the plant was placed.[2]

Each plant was repeatedly lowered six inches onto a cushioned surface, with the process repeated sixty times per plant for the sixty-five plants. Each time the plant would fold its leaves upon descent until a time at which they would not react at all. Some argued that the plants stopped responding due to fatigue rather than learning. But, when each plant was shaken immediately after the sixty drops, they immediately folded their leaves! The drop experiment was conducted week after week and it was found that the plants remembered that the drop was harmless and continued to not react for twenty-eight days. It is clear from the experiment that the plants have some type of memory, and retain that memory for a significant amount of time. There is some intelligence demonstrated by the plant behavior that is occurring without the brain, neurons, or nervous systems of humans and other animals.

Mimicry is another extraordinary ability that some plants possess. Many orchid varieties in particular, will grow to resemble an animal. The Bee Orchid looks like a female bumblebee bee, and emits a sweet scent which male bees mistake for a female and are drawn in to mate. The unwitting bee unknowingly helps pollinate the flower. Over millions of years, natural selection favored bee orchids with traits that effectively attracted male bees, leading to their optimization. This does not indicate that the individual plant consciously decides their appearance or scent. But for plant mimicry to exist, some aspect of Nature has intelligence and decision-making capabilities to adapt to its environment and the life forms with which it interacts. One could argue that this is consciousness–that Nature is conscious.

Beyond plants, the question of consciousness extends to animals. When I think of intelligent animals, elephants come to mind. These majestic creatures have social dynamics within their herds and have long-lasting bonds. They feel empathy, and mourn the loss of a herd member. Elephants are known to hold grudges, seek revenge, and recognize other elephants even after long separations.

The Mirror-Mark Test was developed in 1970 as a gauge of animal self-awareness.[3] Animals who are able to recognize themselves in a mirror and identify a marking that has been put on their body include chimpanzees and orangutans, dolphins, magpies, and fish called cleaner wrasses. So does self-awareness and recognition indicate consciousness?

There is no universally agreed upon definition of consciousness to date that applies to all sentient beings, so we can't actually disregard the consciousness of plants and animals. Per a November 1, 2019 article in *The Conversation*, part of the complexity in defining consciousness is that it cannot be observed.[4] One cannot point to brain structures and state,

"Here is consciousness, here are feelings, here are experiences." The article states that scientists attempt to explain unobservable phenomena by correlating it to something that is observable and quantifiable.

One example is that the sensation of hunger (unobservable), correlates with hypothalamus activity (observable). Similar correlations attempt to tie consciousness to specific brain activity; however, this does not define consciousness. The question of whether something is conscious or not is called "the hard problem of consciousness."

The question of animal (non-human) consciousness is an important one, when we consider the treatment of animals. If certain animals are not conscious, then we may exempt them from ethical considerations and rights. We are then able to question whether these animals have the right to exist on their own terms.[5] That line of thought has made it acceptable to use them for experimentation.

The majority today consider animal testing cruel and unethical, but we still produce enormous quantities of factory-farmed meat. There still exist meat factories with cruel, cramped, and inhumane conditions. The animals are treated as raw materials or inputs in a factory production where output is to be optimized for revenue. As vertebrates with nervous systems, factory-farmed animals undeniably feel pain.

Through observation, we know animals will whimper, lick a wound, or retreat and isolate when experiencing pain. Per the same TedEd video by Robyn J. Cook, lab tests have shown that chicken and rats will self-administer pain medication when hurting.[6] This behavior goes beyond nociception (the body's sense and response to painful stimuli) to a "conscious recognition of harm" involving the brain's interpretation of the stimuli and an adaptive change in behavior.

On the flip side, we can observe an animal feeling pleasure. Dogs, who seem to wear their hearts on their sleeves, are usually very emotive about their joy and excitement. Perhaps they, too, experience qualia. When I'd see my cat luxuriating in a patch of sun near the window, she appears to be experiencing something very pleasant—the qualia of sun beams on her fur. When I pet her and she purrs, there must be a qualia of that desirable experience. Since qualia is subjective conscious experience, perhaps it is evidence of consciousness, and applies to all sentient beings whether or not they display awareness of self.

Our interpretation of an animal's self-awareness depends on our ability to observe it, and is a very human-centric view. According to the December 15, 2021 article in Frontiers in Veterinary Science, titled "Fishnition: Developing Models From Cognition Toward Consciousness," the anthropocentric (humans as the superior species) view of consciousness includes "self-reflection and conceptual categorization."[7] The latter is the understanding of objects in the environment and the role/purpose of these objects. By extension, within this lens, an animal that can group objects as categories is considered conscious. The anthropomorphic (animals as humanlike) view holds that any sensory responsiveness qualifies the animal as conscious. Given the lack of consensus on the definition of consciousness, it challenges rational thought to consider the world and everything in it as conscious.

Let us consider what lies below ground. Beneath the earth lies a vast network—Nature's own internet. Mycelium, the root structure of mushrooms, are the root structures of this network. These mycelial networks have more connections than the human brain, and like neural systems, operate through electrical signals and electrolytes.[8]

The mycelial network monitors nearby plant life, communicates with trees, tracks their nutrition, and distributes nutrients as needed! There is an intelligence at work in this beautiful ecosystem in which plants and trees care for one another. We may argue that mycelia are not conscious, even though they do react to their environment and seem to make decisions in the interest of thriving. Perhaps this misses the point completely—that Nature is intelligent. The extent of what we can do as humans is to understand it, mimic it when inventing our own tools and solutions, and respect that the intricacies of Nature and the natural world are ultimately beyond our control.

Trees have mycorrhizal networks, with root-tip filaments connecting to the mycelial web.[9] Through these connections, fungi and trees sustain their symbiotic relationship. The trees produce sugar through photosynthesis, some of which the fungi consume. In return, the fungi collect nitrogen, phosphorus, and minerals from the soil that trees utilize for life. Young saplings struggling to grow in a shaded area of a forest, where no sunlight is available for photosynthesis, depend on the mycelial-mycorrhizal networks to obtain the nutrients to grow.

Trees also communicate with each other through the air, releasing pheromones to warn neighboring trees about impending danger, such as an approaching giraffe. The neighboring trees start pushing a substance into their leaves that will cause the animal eating its leaves to get sick or even die. Animals like the giraffe have adapted too, sensing the airborne warning gas, and getting to the neighboring tree to eat its leaves before that tree has received a warning!

Once one starts to ponder the intricacies of nature's ecosystems, it's hard not to marvel at the genius of the natural world. Living in California, I've had the privilege of visiting coastal redwood forests many times. These majestic trees grow together and support one another against high winds and other adverse weather. Their shallow root system intertwines and spreads sixty to eighty feet outwards. These trees, known as *Sequoia sempervirens,* grow to three hundred and fifty feet tall, and can live for around two thousand years.[10] They have learned that there is strength in numbers, an example of a natural cooperative community. By intertwining their roots, they create a network that provides mutual support and stability.

All this shows that we share our space with objects both living and inanimate, and countless invisible particles and organisms. We are bathed in a "sea" of intelligent information. Space is also within us. You are a super organism teeming with countless microorganisms and cells that work together to keep you alive. If you recognize that you are a small part of a vast, complex network of organisms, and that you are in a symbiotic relationship with everything in your space—within and without, then you will begin to perceive yourself as part of a vibrant, dynamic whole, interconnected and interdependent.

Loving your space means feeling a deep connection to it. Let your spirit lead you to protect and nurture these spaces, ensuring that they, in turn, nourish you.

We don't know where our soul or spirit resides. We have awareness of something that exists beyond our minds and bodies. *Living beings undeniably possess a certain vitality, whether we call it* sensory awareness or consciousness. Something animates all living beings. Not only that, but every system on Earth is designed to propagate planetary life. According to the Gaia Theory, "this means that life on Earth is a self-regulating system involving the biosphere, the atmosphere, the hydrosphere, and the pedosphere (the skin of soil and living organisms), all of which are intimately integrated as an evolving complex system."[11]

Knowing all we know about the science of our planet, perhaps we should cease the endless cerebral arguments about consciousness and instead experience the Earth as a living, conscious entity. Immerse yourself in first hand experience. Seek wonder, awe, and a deeper connection with the natural world. This is an invitation to know the planet, your Space, through your heart, spirit, and intuition. In Part 6 Chapter 21 which follows, we will discuss choices: how your life is a multitude of choices made and the not-so-obvious factors to consider at every moment of decision.

CHAPTER 20 REFLECTIONS

For years, I have invested in good organic, mold-free coffee that I drink in the morning. There is an entire ritual around filtering the brew, preparing it, smelling it, and the intense pleasure of the very first sip. Coffee evokes all my senses. Other than taste, smell, sight, I'd argue that my hearing is triggered as well with the comfortable "whrrr" of the drink being brewed. All the sensations contribute to my coffee experience. This is the qualia of coffee for me. A while ago, when I was having some acute gut issues I found myself unable to tolerate the caffeine. I felt the loss of qualia experience through the ritual of coffee. I could not successfully substitute with green or herbal tea. It just wasn't the same. I felt sad about it, until I decided to experiment with a new mushroom coffee growing in popularity. The mushroom coffee makers tout their product as a blend of six different mushrooms, some of which help reduce GI inflammation. To my great surprise, I had a qualia experience similar to that of coffee. My ritual was intact, my gut didn't hurt, and I continued to experience the satisfaction of my morning beverage. That's qualia. I can't explain in words the fullness of the simple experience, but it's meaningful enough for me to have sought out a viable substitute.

1. How have you experienced qualia? Here's an example to reflect on: Consider the qualia of your experience with smelling fresh cut grass. You are not identifying

the sight, touch, or even the smell. It is essentially your internal experience of freshly mown grass

2. What is your experience with a plant for which you provide care? How do you relate to the plant's consciousness? If you do not care for any plants, acquire a simple indoor potted plant, like a spider plant. Care for it lovingly, seeking to connect to its consciousness. Notice how you nurture it. Do you talk to it? Do you touch its leaves? Take notice of your internal state, your level of calmness as you interact with the plant

3. Reflect on your relationship with your pet. Pay attention to your inner sensations, your nervous system state as you spend time with your pet. If you do not have a pet, a suggestion is to visit an animal shelter and pet and spend time with a cat or dog

Part 6
Ahead

Live large
Take up space
Be fearless
Know when to watch
And when to act
Life is choice
Life is balance
And compassion is everything
—Smita

Fifteen years ago, I had a nagging sense that I wasn't living as I was meant to. Perhaps the Universe, or my own higher self had designed this ideal life for me. I struggled with chronic illness while raising my children, working full-time, and staying engaged in my family and community. Despite everything, I couldn't shake the feeling that I had fallen short of my potential. I had no idea what that meant in concrete terms, yet I knew I wanted to develop myself further. The words above formed in my mind, as a call to action for myself. This was when I first reckoned with making conscious choices.

I had been shrinking myself, prioritizing everyone else's needs over my own. With my two very young kids, this made sense as they needed so much from me at that stage. But I needed to rethink how I operated in the world—how I saw myself, how I was filled with fear; fear about my health condition, of life's uncertainty, of a world that often felt unfair and cruel. I had, in many ways, become a passive watcher of others' lives. I saw people I knew, or others I did not personally know, push themselves out of their comfort zone, try things, take risks. When did I decide that my fragile health meant I had to play small and "safe"?

As I reflected, I realized that life isn't just about survival—it's about balance and choice. The Well-being Pyramid, a model of balance and alignment within ourselves and our environment, became a guiding principle for me. I realized we always have a choice—we can shrink in fear or step forward with courage. And it is when you keep love in your heart and compassion in your actions then your choices will be stepping stones on a path toward wisdom. The next chapter discusses the deeper choices we all face in every present moment.

CHAPTER 21

The Precious Choice in Every Moment

Love or Fear

In every moment, only the present exists. Spiritual leaders like Eckhart Tolle, Ram Dass, Thich Nhat Hanh, Adyashanti, Buddha, Lao Tzu, and others speak of the present moment as the portal to spiritual awakening. Both spiritual traditions and science agree: neither the past nor the future exists. So, we each have only the present moment, and every moment is a choice.

In each moment, we choose either to contract or to expand our own being —and by extension, the Collective Being . We experience the contraction as fear and the expansion as love. In essence, every moment is a choice between fear and love. One may argue that there are many other emotions that drive the human experience—greed, anger, envy, and many more. But, the underlying driver of all our negative emotions is fear. When anger is expressed, it is a surface emotion. Underneath that is pain, and under the pain is fear. It could be fear of rejection, fear of not being loved, or fear of isolation. Fear exists, and in its absence, love emerges—as happiness, connection, and openness.

> *"There are two basic motivating forces: fear and love. When we are afraid, we pull back from life. When we are in love, we open to all that life has tooffer with passion, excitement, and acceptance."*
> **—John Lennon**

In his book *The Four Agreements*, Don Miguel Ruiz discusses what he refers to as the track of love and the track of fear. Ruiz brings us ancient Toltec wisdom that originated in central Mexico. He teaches that awareness of fear allows us to shift toward love. Ruiz states that love is an action which brings happiness, while fear in action produces suffering.[1]

By tuning inward to thoughts, emotions, and bodily sensations, you can tune into a moment's choice. You can consciously choose a love or fear response in that moment. You must also learn to excavate the underlying emotion in the instance. For example, you may at one moment experience jealousy, anger, or sadness. These are valid emotions, though not the base emotion of fear.

Imagine someone is chosen over you—whether for a relationship or a job. You may experience jealousy, envy or anger. Take a moment to ask yourself.

"Why am I jealous?" I feel that I am better than them. I should have been picked.

"Why is it important to be better than them?" I feel validated for my worthiness.

"Why do you need to feel validated?" So I will know I am valued.

"Why do you need to feel valued by others?" So I will know I belong.

"Why do you need to belong?" Without belonging somewhere, I feel alone.

"What does being alone make you feel?" Afraid.

Thus, we get to the base emotion of fear. Fear is a subtle (or not so subtle) contraction of self—an energetic way to make oneself small. Anger may feel good in the moment. You are expressing, attempting to expand yourself. But anger is not the base emotion. It is a reaction to a deeper pain and an attempt to mitigate it. It is also a way to generate energy for oneself, at least in the moment.

Sit quietly with the anger and feel. Can you get to the underlying pain and hurt of rejection, loss, or abandonment? Feel your pain and the accompanying emotions—perhaps of sadness, disappointment, or even disillusionment. Can you reach your fear and have an honest assessment of what you feel at your core? Contemplate at that moment what it would be like to instead choose a loving and compassionate response, toward yourself and others.

I refrain from categorizing feelings as "good" or "bad" at any given moment, choosing to see them instead as data inputs. Jealousy may not feel expansive to you. An expansive choice, one made in love, feels like an opening up of one's heart space. There is a lightness to a choice of love in each present moment. This is how we grow our consciousness, moment by moment, being only in the present time. Every moment is the opportunity to live in fear or in love. Conscious growth is done in the present moment, with present choices.

Competition or Cooperation

A paradigm shift is reshaping how we regard ourselves and our human experience. We are starting to see ourselves more as spiritual beings living the human experience. Our actions through history have resulted in wars, brutality, purposeful climate degradation, poverty, and suffering that have been manifested from the most fearful parts of us. This kill-or-be-killed mentality has shaped our economic, political, healthcare, and educational systems, embedding competition at their core.

Healthy competition makes us better and gives us some parameters to strive against and push ourselves. Taken too far, we disregard the vulnerable and marginalized members of our global society. Our pursuit of external power often comes at the expense of others' well-being—everyone and everything becomes a commodity. It is reasonable to assume the mindset that created these problems cannot lead us toward conscious growth, evolution, and abundance.

That shift begins with the individual—You. The Well-being Pyramid model encourages you to align with your mind, body, spirit, and space. In plain language, this means you walk the talk. Your beliefs and values are fully aligned with your actions, felt in your spirit as love, spoken to the world as Truth, and you strive to make your space, community, country, world reflect compassion, love, integrity, and equanimity.

Gary Zukav writes in his book, *The Universal Human*, that our souls have several intentions—harmony, cooperation, sharing, and reverence for life. Zukav distinguishes between five-sensory humans—only able to perceive reality through their five senses and are therefore not able to recognize the soul and its intentions, and multi-sensory humans.

Multi-sensory humans are tuned into the subtle cues of the soul, the nuances, the intuitions, the soul's language. Guided by universal truths, multi-sensory humans embrace conscious growth. They are the drivers of our compassion for each other, all beings, and the earth. The shift to a soul or spirit-centered life is one each of us can make.

While some remain unaware, many are awakening to the stark contrast between the world we've built and the one we long for. There is the turmoil we experience in a world we have constructed to be ruthless, competitive, and exploitative of other life. Then there is the yearning for a caring and thoughtful world that nurtures us all. That compassionate world exists as well—within you. Once again, we can choose love instead of fear, by seeking cooperation instead of competition.

The choice lies within you—not in external systems, new leaders, or distant planets. The choice *is* You. If we each embody that choice, the world as we know it will no longer sustain old paradigms. We will reshape every aspect of society, including finance, politics, education, and healthcare, to reflect these intentions.

Solitude or Loneliness

Then stirs the feeling infinite, so felt In solitude, where we are least alone — **Lord Byron**

We are living in a time where anxiety and depression are on the rise. Also, we are lonelier than ever. According to a 2023 Gallup report, 29 percent of the American population have been diagnosed with depression at some point in their lives. Eighteen percent of the population has been or is currently in treatment for depression.[2] Nearly half of the population with depression has been diagnosed with anxiety disorders.[3] In an increasingly challenging world, relentless stressors shape our mental well-being. One such global stressor was the COVID-19 pandemic, whose repercussions continue to affect us today. Anxiety is a very human response to stressors such as this. In many cases, chronic anxiety and depression can lead to social withdrawal, making individuals feel isolated.

At its core, loneliness is a manifestation of fear. As social beings, humans have historically relied on small groups for survival, and abandonment or banishment from the safety of the group threatened that survival. So the fear is primal and understandable through past history. How is this working for us now? Belonging to a group can provide a sense of safety, love, and even purpose within that group. But in today's world that has become increasingly partisan and divided, this type of grouping has often manifested with an insider/outsider mentality. Often, it comes with judgement against the outsiders, and a refusal to accept or make room for ideology or choices that are different from those of our chosen group.

This is a period of great change, as evidenced by the declining role of religion in peoples' lives—to their detriment as some would argue.[4]

Religion has played a vital role in providing community, support, and a salve to loneliness. At their center, all major religions have a spiritual dimension. They aim to strengthen the spiritual cores of its members by providing guidance, community, lessons, and role models. However, in practice, how far has each fallen from its spiritual ideals? If a religion judges or condemns an individual or a particular group, how is that spirituality? If a religion requires one to end another life, how is that a choice of love? Since religion has provided some vital benefits such as belonging, guidance, and support to its followers, those elements can be available within non-religious spiritual practices. We need a spirituality that is global or even cosmic, cherishes all life, provides a sense of deep connection, supports the flourishing of the whole planet, and is all inclusive. It should revere the inner journey of the individual, while supporting the harmony of inner self to the outer world.

Each of us is on a spiritual journey regardless of religion or beliefs. That journey is a solitary one in that it's unique to each person. Choosing to belong to an institution that requires you to squash your own spirit and personal sacred journey is to abandon self. Abandonment of the self is loneliness. So even though you are safely tucked into the folds of a religious community, it is possible to experience profound loneliness.

A January 2024 poll done by the American Psychiatric Association (APA) showed that one in three Americans felt lonely every week in the past year, with 10 percent feeling lonely daily. Young people and single adults were more likely to experience loneliness.[5] These mental states do not bode well for general well-being.

There very often is a spiritual component to anxiety, depression, and loneliness. The sense of disconnect that inevitably arises when experiencing these states can add to one's sense of isolation, and produce a false sense that you are the only one suffering in this manner. Living a spiritual life means being connected to oneself, others, nature, and a higher power. The first step in the transmutation of the isolation of loneliness into the embrace of solitude starts with relationship to self.

This is a kind and compassionate connection to self that promotes inner peace, self-esteem, purpose, empowerment, and hope. Nurture that above all within yourself. From there, you can experience great benefits from the other forms of connection. A nurturing connection with others enables social responsibility, compassion, and healthy relationships. A positive connection with nature entails immersive engagement and identification with the natural world through walks, nurturing plants and animals, observing nature and the night sky. Connection to a higher power or universal consciousness may be expressed through gratitude, prayer, or internal conversations.[6] I would add that dialogue with the universe, i.e., a higher energy, in specific times of my life has had some profound effects for me. I have received help in unexpected ways that further reinforce my relationship with the Universe.

The focus of this book is how to be a balanced, aligned, and well human. Spirituality can be intrinsic to every facet of what makes you You. Core to the spiritual concepts is the idea that spirituality is about connection to oneself, others, the world both natural and human made, and an energy bigger and infinitely more powerful than oneself. That divine connection is how love is felt and expressed. Being alone is not the same as being lonely. One can be alone and never feel lonely if the belief and experience is that we are all connected in a planetary, or even cosmic network of energy. Can you tolerate being alone with your thoughts? Cultivate the ability to feel connection even in solitude.

Some solitude is a necessary part of spiritual growth. In co-creating with the Universe, you are in dialogue with it. You sometimes act and sometimes listen. That is the give and take of your relationship with all that is greater than you. In silence and solitude, wisdom emerges—to inform the beliefs you form and the actions you take.

Boundaries and Boundlessness

The mere act of living in a world of duality means you will encounter contrast. If you have only encountered joy, you cannot truly understand sorrow. You will not have the contrast to help define the exquisiteness and value of joy. I discussed objects and negative space in chapter 13, and explained how the negative space helps define the boundaries and shapes of the objects in that space. Similarly, understanding sorrow and its dimensions and edges helps you define the "shape" of joy. Joy is that much more desirable when one has known the deep depths and contrast of sorrow. Contrast helps us make sense of life.

Just as contrast shapes individual emotions, it also defines the trajectory of human history. As a collective of humans, we are currently living in a time of great contrast. One may contend that it has been this way throughout our history as five-sensory beings motivated mostly by fear. Countries have had great wars, natural disasters, nefarious leaders, but we have also had times of peace, prosperity, and expansion. The contrast of the current time is magnified and includes all of us at once. It is all of humanity intertwined in a global upheaval.

Seeking to define the boundaries of these experiences allows us to find our way to the other side of them. History offers many examples of such extreme contrast, one of the most glaring being Nazi Germany. Much of humanity realized the horror and devastation of the war that occurred. We have that contrast in our collective psyche. We know the "shape" and "form" of that experience. It becomes that much more apparent that the opposite—love and compassion for all humans—is more desirable. This is how humanity has learned on the individual level and as a collective. Thus, boundaries can help us progress.

There has never been a more crucial time in global history to remember the contrast and to thwart the efforts of oppressors who strip people of their human rights, actively oust them from their native lands, and seek to destroy protective laws and constitutions that have been upheld for centuries through misinformation, lies, and deception. True, there is a great deal of positive change needed in existing systems and structures, but that can be done with wisdom, forethought, and organization, instead of with unmitigated greed and a rampant thirst for external power at the expense of all of us.

We have built boundaries between ourselves—geographic, ideological, race-based, gender-based, or some other delineation we have made between what we deem acceptable and what we feel is not. Progressing forward as more evolved and aligned humans means dissolving many of these boundaries. Even as I write this, I feel the heady weight of millennia of thinking and emotion that has been woven into the continued construction of boundaries—yet this must be done.

Doing vs Being

Humanity has always been in the business of Doing. We are restless creatures, striving to make progress—no matter the nature of that progress. Even the ancient hunter-gatherer societies realized then that the tasks essential for their survival were most efficiently completed by delegating the work amongst its members. The early division of labor were the roots of what we have today as a complex, global system of labor and commerce.

The Doing became work and the success metrics for work came to be described by productivity, progress, and growth. Some growth was good, so more growth must be better. With key performance indicators (KPIs) demonstrating progress, organizations have defined their parameters for what constitutes accomplishment in their respective industries. Underlying all of this is the flow of money.

How do insurance companies make money? In the simplest sense, if the amount in premiums paid exceeds the amount in claims paid out, then they have made money. They also invest the money collected in premiums.

How do food companies make money? Well that subject is much more involved than we will address here, but basic economics suggest that the cheaper a company can make a product and the higher the volume of units they sell of that product, the more revenue they stand to make. Other factors like the shelf life of the product or how much of the food is put into a single package will impact the revenue. The relentless drive to extend shelf life has led us down a dark path of harmful preservatives, pesticides, and other chemicals that are linked with cancer, endocrine disruption, developmental issues, and heart disease. For something so vital and basic for human survival, it seems atrocious to cut corners or dupe a consumer with deceptive food marketing just to ensure profits are maximized.

Within this complicated system of commerce and trade lies the individual—you and me. Whether you run organizations or work in one, most of us are invested in staying alive, protecting our loved ones, and optimizing for happiness. We may be exhausted by the effort of keeping up with the business day after day. We may take a momentary reprieve via an annual two-week vacation or one relaxing weekend, bookended by the gerbil wheel of life on either end of the weekend. Is this how we should continue to live and operate in life?

As industries push for greater results, automation has become a primary tool in this pursuit. Enter Artificial Intelligence (AI), a technology often promoted as the answer to productivity concerns—implement AI, and it will leave humans free to do other, more interesting tasks. To some extent, this is proving to be true, as implementing generative AI has indeed resulted in saving time, reducing errors, and automating repetitive tasks. However, many are finding themselves out of jobs due to their company's AI implementations. AI appears to be a force of change that will not be stopped. However, choosing how, when, and to which AI solutions we apply our efforts is crucial.

Currently we have Narrow AI (ANI) and we are moving into the successful implementation of agentic AI, or artificial general intelligence (AGI). Whereas ANI is designed for narrow, specific tasks—like voice recognition or spam filtering—AGI represents a monumental leap. These systems can reason, learn, and perform multiple tasks autonomously, approaching human cognitive ability. Beyond AGI and existing only in theory to date, is artificial super intelligence (ASI). ASI will far surpass human intellectual capability. The grand vision appears to be AI creating and managing AI, such as engagement of whole AI workforces or organizations.

As our technology rapidly evolves, many in leadership are heavily invested in the progress and evolution of AI. What about the growth, expansion, and evolution of humans–the most sophisticated "wetware" we know? That wet technology analogy is mostly referencing the human brain and central nervous system. But, as you have learned in this book, we are so much more than that, and at this point, what is known comprises a fraction of humans' true capabilities. We are underestimating our own true power.

Gaining clarity on your essence, your purpose in this lifetime, and where you can go from here to expand consciousness will not start from anything external to you. The external doing must be supported by times of being. Times of quiet, stillness, and introspection will guide you in accessing your higher mind. It is in the being that the deepest connection to self and to the Universe is realized. That is an experiential journey. Our wisdom traditions teach us about this internal journey, and our spiritual masters have exemplified them. But this is your opportunity to balance the Doing with Being. It is also your birthright as a spiritual being.

The Well-being Pyramid is a conceptual framework you can utilize to fully awaken and align yourself, and also provide balance in your life. As you grow in consciousness, you become more of a person that is increasingly invested in not only individual well-being, but the well-being of all others and of the planet. Let the wisdom gained in the Being inform how you proceed in the Doing as a fully-conscious individual.

For every system and process we have designed and implemented, there are humans with the expertise to champion the necessary improvements. For every "problem" we have, there lies an elegant, compassionate solution. It will take everyone, each of us in this global family, to choose to do their inner work so that they may be appropriately equipped to do the external work of restructuring how we live. We must all realize that well-being is the birthright of all, and that humanity already has all the knowledge and capability to reverse and eliminate its destructive patterns.

As Einstein said, "The most important decision we make is whether we believe we live in a friendly or hostile universe."

A sense of well-being can only truly be fostered if you believe the Universe is here to support you and desires your highest vibrational state. Your relationship with your mind, body, spirit, and space—through which you are intimately and cosmically connected to all of consciousness—is the way toward your whole being's well-being. You, as a spiritual being, exert influence over all others. When your energy is high, it invites others to rise to a higher frequency as well.

It can be daunting to think about all the positive external change we would like to see in the world, coupled with the weighty question of how to do it. I assure you that the answer to how we can make these changes will come. It will be done by spirit-aligned beings in every facet of life, seeking peace and well-being, making changes at all levels, top down and bottom up. Change does truly start with the individual. Change yourself to change your world.

Our path to love is through fear. By going through it, we transcend it. I feel we are on that evolutionary trajectory and our collective awareness is growing. The human collective is simply each of us living through this time. Be the change we so desperately need in the world. Be a fully aligned human and attend to your well-being. All change starts within and radiates from there. Your consciously elevated thoughts and actions help create a new world that reflects those thoughts and actions. This can only happen with aligned, wise, and well humans.

WISDOM IN CHAOTIC TIMES

"The human soul is on its journey from the law to love, from discipline to liberation, from the moral plane to the spiritual." — **Rabindranath Tagore**

True wisdom is acquired through the experience and study of life–your life, the lives of others, and planetary life. Everything that is required for your growth is presented to you in the form of people, experiences, challenges, and pain. In an exquisitely orchestrated dance, we and the Universe co-conspire for our evolution. Such is the nature of creation, and we are all a part of it.

Conscious growth and expansion is the recognition and active participation in your life path and learning. It is the opposite of an unconscious and reactive life, an unexamined life. I wrote this book to convey to you how sacred your life truly is and to provide a framework for inner and outer peace and alignment. *The Aligned Human* facilitates that growth by providing a deep understanding of authentic, whole-being well-being and awakening.

You have everything you need to take control of your well-being despite the grave and pressing issues of these uncertain times and also because of them. This chaotic era, with its volatility, upheaval, and devastation, is playing out with a purpose—to provide the necessary contrast to mobilize great change and healing. Contrast, as we have described in this book, teaches through duality. The experience of war—violence, coercion, conflict, power agendas—strengthens the case and argument for peace.

Our shadow selves, the suppressed and hidden pieces of our being, have so much to offer as insight into ourselves. As an example, this could be illustrated through an often heard phrase these days–toxic positivity. Toxic positivity is the expression of positive statements in response to a hardship or difficult challenge, with the intention of minimizing or negating the associated emotions. One engaging in toxic positivity is repressing any negative feelings instead of expressing, processing, and moving through those feelings.

Shadow work can effectively address toxic positivity. Here one would examine why these authentic but difficult feelings are being repressed, because there is a deeper, underlying driver to that choice. Wisdom is cultivated through self-reflection and understanding the shadows from which we hide. Dr. Laura Gabayan, a former ER doctor at UCLA, a researcher, and the author of *Common Wisdom, 8 Scientific Elements of a Meaningful Life.*[7] Gabayan found through countless interviews of ordinary people that there are eight traits of the wise: resilience, kindness, positivity, spirituality, humility, tolerance, creativity, and curiosity. Gabayan describes each trait.

- Resilience - tenacity to gracefully weather the ups and downs of life with grace
- Kindness - desire for deep connection and belonging
- Positivity - ability to find joy during even difficult times, things happen for you not to you
- Spirituality - a belief there is something greater than you
- Humility - a growth mindset, a beginner's mind
- Tolerance - compassion for all
- Creativity - a drive to create new visions with fresh perspective

- Curiosity - ability to embrace life with awe and wonder

Through presenting the Well-being Pyramid framework, *The Aligned Human* demonstrates the characteristics of wisdom. These can be exercised and made true to you. It is wise humans who will help navigate through these chaotic times to a future in which we are all awakened, aligned, and living a life of authentic well-being and deep mutual respect.

Wisdom is like qualia—hard to define. But if you seek it, you'll know when it is present. It is a knowing, an understanding of a much wider perspective. Wisdom may come like a gentle rain, filling up your spirit and aligning you to your higher self, but will you recognize and embrace it? Will it get your attention? Our wise leaders, past and present, have selflessly shared their knowledge, should you choose to discover. They are compassionate souls who put forth their offerings of elevated perspectives, never pushing the agenda upon you. The wise know that wisdom cannot be given or taken to be understood. It must be wholeheartedly and internally realized and chosen. That speaks to the essence of our truth—that free will is fundamental to each of us. And that is an individual choice that comes from insight.

Insight, per Merriam-Webster, is "the act or result of apprehending the inner nature of things or of seeing intuitively". Insight comes from reflecting on one's experiences. Thus wisdom, ageless and therefore accessible to anyone, is gained experientially. Why are those experiences so often through suffering? Pain is elemental to life on this planet. If we choose, pain will teach us. Whereas suffering is a subjective and on some level a rejection of what is happening to us, and a judgement that this anguish should not be happening to us, pain is an objective assessment of the experience.

I have lived almost half my life in some level of chronic physical pain. Chronic pain is a relentless beast, but when I finally accepted that this is me and pain is a part of it (which has taken some years!), the psychological suffering diminished. I began to see pain as part of my larger purpose.

When we accept the pain and stop denying its existence or pushing against it in an effort to overcome it, we have the opportunity to be fully present with reality. Only in the present is wisdom gained. We can then intimately understand the pain and why we have chosen to suffer. We can see ourselves through a deeply compassionate lens. That perspective also allows us to see into the suffering of others and empathetically understand. With that wisdom, we can take actions to alleviate suffering—for ourselves and for others. Wisdom in action will lead us to a future world of well-aligned humans.

IN CONCLUSION

Fractals are never-ending, recursive patterns that repeat independent of scale. This makes them infinitely complex. Both Nature and the human body contain fractals. The bronchial tree within our lungs, our blood vessels within the circulatory system–branching from larger vessels, to increasingly smaller vessels, to the capillaries, and the fractal patterns of the neuron's axons and dendrites within the human brain are just a few examples of this. In the natural world our water ways with its oceans, lakes, rivers, tributaries, and small streams are fractal in composition. Broccoli florets grow in a fractal pattern. Succulents and tree branches are evident of fractals in nature. The list is quite endless and awe-inspiring when we regard this as evidence of the intelligence and beauty of the natural world and our own selves as extensions of nature.

At a larger scale, the way human society organizes demonstrates fractals at play. We are part of ever-larger social units from family, to community, to larger organizations. We are able to recognize repeating patterns and model highly complex systems by leveraging fractals. AI utilizes fractal principles in recognizing patterns. modeling complex systems, and analyzing data.

The sophisticated, elegant, and organizing principles inherent in so many examples within us and around us in the natural world are indicative of how connected we are to all that is around us. We are Nature, ever-connected to the deeper intelligence of infinite processes that are much bigger than the small, separate selves we often accept ourselves to be. What we do—to others, plant and animal life, the Earth—with the technology we develop, we do to ourselves. Recognizing and valuing this inherent connection is the starting point of true wisdom and a core message of this book.

The Aligned Human started with a question: "How do we choose to observe ourselves, course-correct, and align for health, abundance, and well-being, and, in doing so, evolve to become better versions of ourselves?" The book was written to remind you that your life is to be experienced and fully embodied. Your life contains the lessons you need to grow. The Well-being Pyramid was discussed in detail as a framework for achieving greater alignment and well-being within your life. The steps you take to enhance your mind, body, spirit, and space and to integrate as a well-aligned human contribute positively to your path of greater wisdom.

We need wise and aligned beings more than ever in today's world of uncertainty, injustice, fear, and separation. We need humans who understand the important choices we face as we shape and form our future world. This is a call to action for you to recognize that you are free to choose love over fear, cooperation and collaboration over exploitation and competition, and healthy boundaries over those that separate and exclude. We have come to a collective turning point—a crossroads. What we opt for now will forever define what it means to be human. Let us strive for the word "human" to convey beings who recognize the wisdom of who they truly are and choose to embody the best qualities, the most positive attributes of humankind. Let our history include how we transmuted the precarious circumstances we find ourselves in during these chaotic times through profound growth and wisdom. Let future generations celebrate us as their ancestors who had the insight, strength, and love to consider and value them, the youngest members of humankind and those yet to be born. The time is now; the future is now. Well-aligned humans will change the world.

Notes

Introduction

1. "Global Life Expectancy to Increase by Nearly 5 Years by 2050 despite Geopolitical, Metabolic, and Environmental Threats," *ScienceDaily*, May 17, 2024, https://www.sciencedaily.com/releases/2024/05/240517164149.htm.

2. World Health Organization, *World Health Statistics 2024: Monitoring Health for the SDGs, Sustainable Development Goals* (Geneva: World Health Organization, May 21, 2024), https://www.who.int/publications/i/item/9789240094703.

3. Global Wellness Institute, "What Is Wellness?" *Global Wellness Institute*, https://globalwellnessinstitute.org/what-is-wellness/. Accessed April 20, 2025.

Chapter 1

1. "About Richard," *The Barrett Academy*, https://www.barrettacademy.com/about-richard. Accessed April 20, 2025.

2. Kendra Cherry, MSEd, "Abraham Maslow Is the Founder of Humanistic Psychology," *Verywell Mind*, February 10, 2025, https://www.verywellmind.com/biography-of-abraham-maslow-1908-1970-2795524.

3. Elizabeth Hopper, "Maslow's Hierarchy of Needs Explained," *ThoughtCo*, May 14, 2024, https://www.thoughtco.com/maslows-hierarchy-of-needs-4582571.

4. Henry J. Venter, "Maslow's Self-Transcendence: How It Can Enrich Organization Culture and Leadership," *International Journal of Business, Humanities and Technology* 2, no. 7 (December 2012).

Chapter 2

1. "Homo Sapiens | The Smithsonian Institution's Human Origins Program," *What Does It Mean to be Human?*, accessed April 21, 2025, https://humanorigins.si.edu/evidence/human-fossils/species/homo-sapiens.

2. Brian Handwerk, "An Evolutionary Timeline of Homo Sapiens," *Smithsonian.com*, February 2, 2021, https://www.smithsonianmag.com/science-nature/essential-timeline-understanding-evolution-homo-sapiens-180976807/.

3. Erin Blakemore, "What Was the Neolithic Revolution?" *National Geographic*, April 5, 2019, https://www.nationalgeographic.com/culture/article/neolithic-agricultural-revolution.

4. Beata Souders, MSc, "What Motivates People? Exploring Human Behavior," *PositivePsychology.com*, March 11, 2025, https://positivepsychology.com/motivation-human-behavior/.

5. Steve Taylor, "The Power of Purpose," *Psychology Today*, July 21, 2013, https://www.psychologytoday.com/us/blog/out-the-darkness/201307/the-power-purpose.

6. C.D. Ryff, "Psychological Well-Being Revisited: Advances in the Science and Practice of Eudaimonia," *Psychotherapy and Psychosomatics* 83, no. 1 (2014): 10-28, https://doi.org/10.1159/000353263. Epub November 19, 2013. PMID: 24281296; PMCID: PMC4241300.

7. Tchiki Davis, "Self Actualization: Definition, Needs, Examples, and Tips," *The Berkeley Well-Being Institute*, accessed April 20, 2025, https://www.berkeleywellbeing.com/self-actualization.html.

8. Michael Singer, "Stages of the Spiritual Path - A Continuum of Letting Go," *The Michael Singer Podcast*, produced by Sounds True, April 9, 2022, podcast, YouTube video, 49:46, https://www.youtube.com/watch?v=W23Qob0d6rA.

Chapter 3

1. Michelle Faverio, "Teens, Social Media and Technology 2024," *Pew Research Center*, December 12, 2024, https://www.pewresearch.org/internet/2024/12/12/teens-social-media-and-technology-2024/.

2. "Mental Health by the Numbers," *NAMI*, March 27, 2025, https://www.nami.org/about-mental-illness/mental-health-by-the-numbers/#:~:text=5.5%25%20of%20U.S.%20adults%20experienced,represents%201%20in%2020%20adults.

3. "Four Parts of the Mind," *Sadhguru Wisdom*, https://www.sadhguruwisdom.org/wisdom/four-parts-of-the-mind-a-yogic-perspective/. Accessed April 21, 2025.

4. Alexandra Keeler, "We All Get 'Monkey Mind' - and Neuroscience Supports the Buddhist Solution," *Big Think*, March 3, 2023, https://bigthink.com/neuropsych/we-all-get-monkey-mind-and-neuroscience-supports-the-buddhist-solution/.

5. Dan Harris, et al., *Meditation for Fidgety Skeptics: A 10% Happier How-to Book* (London: Yellow Kite, 2020).

6. David Robson, "Don't Fret, Neurotics – There Are Advantages to Worrying," *The Guardian*, Guardian News and Media, July 16, 2023, https://www.theguardian.com/science/2023/jul/16/dont-fret-neurotics-there-are-advantages-to-worrying.

7. Lynn Zubernis, "Why Does Watching Dystopian Shows Feel so Good?" *Psychology Today*, Sussex Publishers, October 1, 2022, https://www.psychologytoday.com/us/blog/the-science-fandom/202210/why-does-watching-dystopian-shows-feel-so-good.

8. Emilia Kirk, "The Attention Economy: Standing out among the Noise," *Forbes*, Forbes Magazine,

March 23, 2022, https://www.forbes.com/councils/
forbesbusinessdevelopmentcouncil/2022/03/23/the-attentio
n-economy-standing-out-among-the-noise/.

9. Ira Bedzow, "How to Break Free from the Attention Economy,"
    Forbes, Forbes Magazine, September 7, 2022, https://www.
    forbes.com/sites/irabedzow/2022/09/07/how-to-break-fre
    e-from-the-attention-economy/?sh=772df72e6753.

10. Kendra Cherry, "How Social Comparison Theory
    Influences Our Views on Ourselves," *Verywell Mind*, May
    21, 2024, https://www.verywellmind.com/what-is-the-socia
    l-comparison-process-2795872.

11. Eric Barker, "How to Overcome Fomo: Fear of Missing
    Out," *Time*, June 7, 2016, https://time.com/4358140/
    overcome-fomo/.

12. "Fomo Is Real: How the Fear of Missing Out Affects Your
    Health," *Cleveland Clinic*, August 23, 2023, https://health.
    clevelandclinic.org/understanding-fomo.

13. Brene Brown, "Brene Brown on Blame," *RSA*, February
    3, 2015, video, 1:04, https://www.youtube.com/
    watch?v=RZWf2_2L2v8.

14. Catherine Cote, "Growth Mindset vs. Fixed Mindset: What's
    the Difference?" *Business Insights Blog*, March 10, 2022, https://
    online.hbs.edu/blog/post/growth-mindset-vs-fixed-mindset.

15. Ashley Carucci, "All-or-Nothing Thinking: Examples,
    Effects, and How to Manage," *Psych Central*,
    August 22, 2022, https://psychcentral.com/health/
    all-or-nothing-thinking-examples.

Chapter 4

1. "Neuralink's First Human Patient Shares His Experience," *KVUE*, May 17, 2024, video, 1:52, https://www.youtube. com/watch?v=IbM4-rcujxY&t=40s.

2. "Pioneering Brain Computer Interfaces," *Neuralink*, https:// neuralink.com/. Accessed April 21, 2025.

3. "AI Risks That Could Lead to Catastrophe: Cais," *AI Risks That Could Lead to Catastrophe | CAIS*, https://www.safe.ai/ ai-risk. Accessed April 21, 2025.

4. Bernard Marr, "10 Wonderful Examples of Using Artificial Intelligence (AI) for Good," *Forbes*, February 20, 2024, https://www.forbes.com/sites/bernardmarr/2020/06/22/1 0-wonderful-examples-of-using-a

5. Peter H. Diamandes, "Why AI Matters And How To Deal With The Coming Change w/ Emad Mostaque," produced by PHD Ventures, *Moonshots with Peter Diamandes*, June 29, 2023, podcast, YouTube video, 31:00, https://www.youtube. com/watch?v=ciX_iFGyS0M.

6. Khan Academy, *Khan Academy*, https://www.khanacademy. org/. Accessed April 21, 2025.

7. "Meet Khanmigo: Khan Academy's AI-Powered Teaching Assistant & Tutor," *Meet Khanmigo: Khan Academy's AI-Powered Teaching Assistant & Tutor*, https://www.khanmigo. ai/. Accessed April 21, 2025.

8. Eugene Klishevich, "How AI Is Expanding the Mental Health Market," *Forbes*, June 25, 2024, https://www.forbes.com/ councils/forbestechcouncil/2024/06/25/how-ai-is-expandin g-the-mental-health-market/.

9. Woebot Health, *Woebot Health*, https://woebothealth.com/. Accessed April 21, 2025.

10. "Ollie AI: AI-Powered Employee Support for Global Enterprises," *Ollie AI | AI-Powered Employee Support for Global Enterprises*, https://www.ollie.health/. Accessed April 21, 2025.

11. "Your Emotional Health Assistant," *Youper*, https://www.youper.ai/. Accessed April 21, 2025.

12. Anoushka Thakkar et al., "Artificial Intelligence in Positive Mental Health: A Narrative Review," *Frontiers in Digital Health* 6 (March 18, 2024), https://doi.org/10.3389/fdgth.2024.1280235.

13. Vivek Hallegere Murthy. *Together: The Healing Power of Human Connection in a Sometimes Lonely World.* Harper Wave\, an Imprint of HarperCollinsPublishers, 2023.

14. Lexie Pelchen, "Internet Usage Statistics in 2025," *Forbes*, Forbes Magazine, March 1, 2024, www.forbes.com/home-improvement/internet/internet-statistics/.

15. "Replika," *Replika.com*, accessed April 21, 2025, replika.com/.

16. Will Kenton, "Conscious Capitalism: Definition, 4 Principles, and Company Examples," *Investopedia*, January 5, 2024, www.investopedia.com/terms/c/conscious-capitalism.asp.

17. Alan Moore, *Watchmen* (DC Comics, 2013).

Chapter 5

1. Jeremy Sutton, Mihály Csíkszentmihályi: The Father of Flow, *PositivePsychology.com*, March 31, 2025, https://positivepsychology.com/mihaly-csikszentmihalyi-father-of-flow/.

2. Caroline Leaf, "How Are the Mind & the Brain Different? A Neuroscientist Explains," *Mindbodygreen*, March 8, 2021, https://www.mindbodygreen.com/articles/difference-between-mind-and-brain-neuroscientist.

3. Tenku Ruff et al., "How Can Buddhism Help with Grief?" *Lion's Roar*, accessed April 22, 2025, https://www.lionsroar. com/how-buddhism-helps-with-grief/#:~:text=Tenku%20 Ruff%3A%20Grief%20is%20not,no%20one%20can%20 tell%20us.

4. Barbara Sahakian, Jacquelyn Langley, and Christelle Langley, "How Antidepressants, Ketamine and Psychedelic Drugs May Make Brains More Flexible – New Research," *The Conversation*, October 23, 2023, https://theconversation. com/how-antidepressants-ketamine-and-psychedelic-drug s-may-make-brains-more-flexible-new-research-216025.

5. Gil Fronsdal, "The Buddha's Eightfold Path," *Insight Meditation Center*, September 25, 2012, https://www. insightmeditationcenter.org/2012/09/article-the-buddha s-eightfold-path/.

6. "Transcendental Meditation Technique – Official Website," *Transcendental Meditation Technique – Official Website*, accessed April 22, 2025, https://www.tm.org/.

7. Colleen Elder, Sanford Nidich, Frances Moriarty, and Reibecca Nidich, "Effect of Transcendental Meditation on Employee Stress, Depression, and Burnout: A Randomized Controlled Study," *The Permanente Journal* 18, no. 1 (Winter 2014): 19-23, https://doi.org/10.7812/TPP/13-102.

8. Fred Travis, Linda Valosek, Alexander Konrad IV, James Link, John Salerno, Robert Scheller, and Sanford Nidich, "Effect of Meditation on Psychological Distress and Brain Functioning: A Randomized Controlled Study," *Brain and Cognition* 125 (August 2018): 100 105, https://doi. org/10.1016/j.bandc.2018.03.011.

9. Caroline Jammes, Iris Heiman, and Hakima Amri, "A Pilot Intervention to Reduce Burnout and Enhance Resilience through Transcendental Meditation among Georgetown University Medical Students," *BMC Medical Education*

25, no. 1 (April 3, 2025): 478, https://doi.org/10.1186/
s12909-025-07004-1.

Chapter 6

1. Paul Frysh, "How Little Doses of Sunlight Help the
   Body," *WebMD*, March 10, 2024, https://www.webmd.
   com/a-to-z-guides/ss/slideshow-sunlight-health-effects.

2. "What Is Earthing," *Earthing Institute*, accessed April 22,
   2025, https://earthinginstitute.net/what-is-earthing/.

Chapter 7

1. Jean-Philippe Vert, "Unlocking the Mysteries of Complex
   Biological Systems with Agentic AI," *MIT Technology
   Review*, November 13, 2024, https://www.technologyreview.
   com/2024/11/13/1106750/unlocking-the-mysteries-o
   f-complex-biological-systems-with-agentic-ai/.

2. "Systems Theory," *The Jolly Contrarian*, accessed
   April 23, 2025, https://jollycontrarian.com/index.
   php?title=Systems_theory.

3. "What Is Systems Biology?" *Institute for Systems Biology
   (ISB)*, accessed April 23, 2025, https://isbscience.org/
   what-is-systems-biology/.

Chapter 8

1. Livia Gershon, "A Brief History of the Calorie,"
   JSTOR Daily, February 6, 2020, https://daily.jstor.
   org/a-brief-history-of-the-calorie/.

2. "Fast Food Global Forecast Report 2025: Market Will
   Reach a Staggering $1.25 Trillion by 2033, Driven by
   Increasing Number of Quick Service Restaurants (QSR)

in Developed and Developing Nations," *Business Wire*, January 23, 2025, https://www.businesswire.com/news/home/20250123822178/en/Fast-Food-Global-Forecast-Report-2025-Market-Will-Reach-a-Staggering-%241.25-Trillion-by-2033-Driven-by-Increasing-Number-of-Quick-Service-Restaurants-QSR-in-Developed-and-Developing-Nations---ResearchAndMarkets.com.

3. Daisy A. John and Giridhara R. Babu, "Lessons from the Aftermaths of Green Revolution on Food System and Health," *Frontiers in Sustainable Food Systems* 5 (2021): 644559, https://doi.org/10.3389/fsufs.2021.644559.

4. Kobad Bhavnagri, "Sustainable Agriculture Is the New Green Revolution," *BloombergNEF*, 9 Mar. 2023, about.bnef.com/blog/sustainable-agriculture-is-the-new-green-revolution/.

5. "Food Additives," *World Health Organization*, 16 Nov. 2023, www.who.int/news-room/fact-sheets/detail/food-additives.

6. Olivia Backhaus and Melanie Benesh, "EWG Analysis: Almost All New Food Chemicals Greenlighted by Industry, Not the FDA," *Environmental Working Group,* 13 Apr. 2022, www.ewg.org/news-insights/news/2022/04/ewg-analysis-almost-all-new-food-chemicals-greenlighted-industry-not-fda.

7. "Generally Recognized as Safe (GRAS)," *U.S. Food and Drug Administration*, FDA, 17 Oct. 2023, www.fda.gov/food/food-ingredients-packaging/generally-recognized-safe-gras#:~:text=%22GRAS%22%20is%20an%20acronym%20for,phrase%20Generally%20Recognized%20As%20Safe.

8. Iris Myers, "EWG's Dirty Dozen Guide to Food Chemicals: The Top 12 to Avoid | Environmental Working Group," *Environmental Working Group*, EWG, 18 Mar. 2025, www.ewg.org/consumer-guides/ewgs-dirty-dozen-guide-food-chemicals-top-12-avoid.

9. Nicole F. Roberts, "Americans Sit More than Anytime in History and It's Literally Killing Us," *Forbes*, Forbes Magazine, 6 Mar. 2019, www.forbes.com/sites/nicolefisher/2019/03/06/americans-sit-more-than-anytime-in-history-and-its-literally-killing-us/?sh=2fa49ce5779d.

10. Dan Buettner, *The Blue Zones Solution: Eating and Living like the World's Healthiest People* (Washington, DC: National Geographic, 2015).

11. Kannan Ramar, et al., "Sleep is Essential to Health: An American Academy of Sleep Medicine Position Statement," *Journal of Clinical Sleep Medicine* 17, no. 10 (Oct. 1, 2021): 2115–19, https://doi.org/10.5664/jcsm.9476.

12. National Institute of Neurological Disorders and Stroke, "Brain Basics: Understanding Sleep," National Institutes of Health, accessed April 28, 2025, https://www.ninds.nih.gov/health-information/public-education/brain-basics/brain-basics-understanding-sleep.

13. "Relaxation Techniques: Try These Steps to Lower Stress," *Mayo Clinic*, Mayo Foundation for Medical Education and Research, www.mayoclinic.org/healthy-lifestyle/stress-management/in-depth/relaxation-technique/art-20045368. Accessed April 23, 2025.

Chapter 9

1. Mary Fairchild, "Why Is the Holy Spirit the Least Understood Member of the Trinity?" *Learn Religions*, Learn Religions, May 7, 2019, www.learnreligions.com/who-is-the-holy-spirit-701504.

2. "Difference between Soul & Spirit," *Paramahamsa Vishwananda*, published June 12, 2016, YouTube video, 3:25, https://www.youtube.com/watch?v=x7ZWAwkP9zo.

3. Stephen Elliott, "On the Immortality of the Soul." *Foundations*, 2013, foundations.vision.org/immortality-soul-149.

4. Michael Lipka, Michael, Patricia Tevington, and Kelsey Jo Starr. "8 Facts about Atheists." *Pew Research Center*, Pew Research Center, 7 Feb. 2024, www.pewresearch.org/short-reads/2024/02/07/8-facts-about-atheists/.

5. Katherine Swancutt, "Animism." *Open Encyclopedia of Anthropology*, 25 June 2019, www.anthroencyclopedia.com/entry/animism.

Chapter 10

1. Mark Leary, "What Is the Ego, and Why Is It so Involved in My Life?" *Psychology Today*, Sussex Publishers, 13 May 2019, www.psychologytoday.com/us/blog/toward-a-less-egoic-world/201905/what-is-the-ego-and-why-is-it-so-involved-in-my-life.

2. The Seat of the Soul Institute. *Seatofthesoul.com*. Accessed 23 Apr. 2025.

3. *The Untethered Soul & The Surrender Experiment - Official Site.* Untetheredsoul.com/michael-singer. Accessed 23 Apr. 2025.

Chapter 11

1. Gregg Levoy, "Synchronicities: A Sure Sign You're on the Right Path," *Psychology Today*, Sussex Publishers, December 19, 2017, https://www.psychologytoday.com/us/blog/passion/201712/synchronicities-sure-sign-youre-the-right-path.

2. Zawn Villines, "What Are Chakras? Concept, Origins, and Effect on Health." *Medical News Today*, MediLexicon International, 20 Nov. 2023, www.medicalnewstoday.com/articles/what-are-chakras-concept-origins-and-effect-on-health.

3. Anita Chen Marshall, "Traditional Chinese Medicine and Clinical Pharmacology." Edited by Franz J. Hock and Michael R. Gralinski. *Drug Discovery and Evaluation: Methods in Clinical Pharmacology*, U.S. National Library of Medicine, 2 Mar. 2020, pmc.ncbi.nlm.nih.gov/articles/PMC7356495/.

4. Tianjun Liu, "The Scientific Hypothesis of an 'Energy System' in the Human Body," *Journal of Traditional Chinese Medical Sciences* 5, no. 1 (January 2018): 29–34, https://doi.org/10.1016/j.jtcms.2018.02.003.

5. Ashley Welch, "What Is Energy Healing?" *EverydayHealth.com*, July 11, 2023, www.everydayhealth.com/integrative-health/energy-healing/guide/.

6. Joe Dispenza, "Changing Energy Is Easier Than Changing Matter," produced by Heal with Kelly, *HEAL with Kelly Podcast*, September 4, 2022, podcast, YouTube video, 13:41, https://www.youtube.com/watch?v=hjKEy6xoMbA.

7. Deepak Chopra, "The Quantum Body: How Our Thoughts and Emotions Influence Us and the World," produced by The Chopra Well, YouTube video, 15:32, https://www.youtube.com/watch?v=V70KSWfemys.

Chapter 12

1. Mark Hyman, *Food Fix: How to Save Our Health, Our Economy, Our Communities, and Our Planet – One Bite at a Time* (New York: Little, Brown Spark, 2022).

2. "Climate Change," *World Health Organization*, October 12, 2023, www.who.int/news-room/fact-sheets/detail/climate-change-and-health.

3. Andrea Miller and Lindsey Jacobson, "Behind the Looming Soil Shortage," *CNBC*, June 5, 2022, www.cnbc.com/video/2022/06/05/behind-the-looming-soil-shortage.html.

4. Laila Benkrima, "Ultra-processed foods are not only bad for our bodies, their production damages our environments," *The Conversation*, September 24, 2023, https://theconversation. com/ultra-processed-foods-are-not-only-bad-for-our-bodie s-their-production-damages-our-environments-211815.

5. Christy Clutter, "Disappearance of the Human Microbiota: How We May Be Losing Our Oldest Allies," *American Society for Microbiology*, November 8, 2019, https://asm. org/articles/2019/november/disappearance-of-the-gu t-microbiota-how-we-may-be.

6. Aristo Vojdani et al., "Environmental Triggers and Autoimmunity," *Autoimmune Diseases* 2014 (2014): 798029, https://doi.org/10.1155/2014/798029.

7. Datis Kharrazian, "Exposure to Environmental Toxins and Autoimmune Conditions," *Integrative Medicine: A Clinician's Journal* 20, no. 2 (April 2021): 20–24, https://pmc.ncbi.nlm. nih.gov/articles/PMC8325494/.

8. Danuta Witkowska, Joanna Słowik, and Karolina Chilicka, "Heavy Metals and Human Health: Possible Exposure Pathways and the Competition for Protein Binding Sites," *Molecules* 26, no. 19 (October 7, 2021): 6060, https://doi. org/10.3390/molecules26196060.

9. American Thyroid Association, "Press Room," accessed April 25, 2025, https://www.thyroid.org/media-main/press-room/.

10. The Dr. Hyman Show, "Heavy Metals And Health: The Untold Story," *YouTube*, February 15, 2021, https://www. youtube.com/watch?v=73piAhxmDGY.

11. Louise Morales-Brown, "Chelation Therapy: Definition, Benefits, and Risks," *Medical News Today*, September 3, 2020, https://www.medicalnewstoday.com/articles/chelation-therapy.Medical News Today

12. "Greenwashing in the Food Industry: What Is It and How Can You Avoid It?" *FoodCycler*, April 22, 2022. https://foodcycler.com/blogs/sustainability/greenwashing-in-the-foo d-industry-what-is-it-and-how-can-you-avoid-it.

13. Adam Hayes, "Fast Fashion: How It Impacts Retail Manufacturing," *Investopedia*, published approximately 10 months ago, https://www.investopedia.com/terms/f/fast-fashion.asp.Investopedia

14. Tonya Mosley, "Is 'Toxic Fashion' Making Us Sick? A Look at the Chemicals Lurking in Our Clothes," *NPR*, July 19, 2023, https://www.npr.org/2023/07/19/1188343293/is-toxi c-fashion-making-us-sick-a-look-at-the-chemicals-lurk ing-in-our-clothes.

15. Victoria Masterson, "9 Ways AI Is Helping Tackle Climate Change," *World Economic Forum*, February 12, 2024, https://www.weforum.org/stories/2024/02/ ai-combat-climate-change/.

16. Shaolei Ren and Adam Wierman, "The Uneven Distribution of AI's Environmental Impacts," *Harvard Business Review*, July 15, 2024, https://hbr.org/2024/07/the-uneven-distributio n-of-ais-environmental-impacts.

17. Dara Kerr and A Martínez, "Tech Companies Look to Renewable Energy to Power AI," *NPR*, October 29, 2024, https://www.npr.org/2024/10/29/nx-s1-5161411/tec h-companies-look-to-renewable-energy-to-power-ai.

18. Koti Spandana, "How Harmful Is TBHQ?" *MedicineNet*, August 12, 2021, https://www.medicinenet.com/ how_harmful_is_tbhq/article.htm.

Chapter 13

1. Kira Schabram, Matt Bloom, and Denis "DJ" DiDonna, "Research: The Transformative Power of Sabbaticals," *Harvard*

Business Review, February 22, 2023, https://hbr.org/2023/02/research-the-transformative-power-of-sabbaticals.

2. Rosie McCall, "The Human Body Is 99 Percent Empty Space – So Why Can't We Walk Through Walls?" *IFLScience*, July 18, 2017, https://www.iflscience.com/the-human-body-is-99-percent-empty-space-so-why-cant-we-walk-through-walls-47375.

3. Ethan Siegel, "Empty Space Has More Energy Than Everything in the Universe Combined," *Big Think*, January 29, 2014, https://bigthink.com/starts-with-a-bang/empty-space-has-more-energy-than-everything-in-the-universe-combined/.

4. Meghan Bartels, "Does Dark Energy Change over Time?" *Scientific American*, April 12, 2024, https://www.scientificamerican.com/article/does-dark-energy-change-over-time/.

5. Will Kenton, "Web 2.0 vs. Web 3.0," *Investopedia*, August 8, 2024, https://www.investopedia.com/web-20-web-30-5208698.

Chapter 14

1. "A Brief History of Interior Design," *Interior Designers for Legislation in New York (IDLNY)*, accessed April 25, 2025, https://www.idlny.org/history-of-interior-design.

2. Pat Tompkins, "18 Astounding Ancient Ruins to Visit Around the World," *AFAR*, December 6, 2024, https://www.afar.com/magazine/incredible-ancient-ruins-to-see-around-the-world.

3. "Everything About Derinkuyu Underground City: The History and Today in 2023," *Cappadocia Travel Pass*, January 20, 2023, https://cappadociatravelpass.com/everything-about-derinkuyu-underground-city-the-history-and-today-in-2023.

4. Gill Hale, Stella Martin, and Josephine De Winter, *The Feng Shui Home: Creating Spiritual Spaces in Your Environment with Altars and Shrines, Space Clearing and the Ancient Chinese Art of Feng Shui* (London: Duncan Baird Publishers, 2001).

5. "Taoism - an overview," *ScienceDirect Topics*, accessed April 25, 2025, https://www.sciencedirect.com/topics/social-sciences/taoism.

6. Robert Boyd and Peter J. Richerson, "Culture and the Evolution of Human Cooperation," *Philosophical Transactions of the Royal Society B: Biological Sciences* 364, no. 1533 (2009): 3281–3288, https://www.ncbi.nlm.nih.gov/pmc/articles/PMC2781880/.

7. "The Costs and Benefits of Tribalism," *Quillette*, April 9, 2022, https://quillette.com/2022/04/09/the-costs-and-benefits-of-tribalism/.

8. United Nations Development Programme, "10 Things to Know About Indigenous Peoples," *UNDP Stories*, July 29, 2021, https://stories.undp.org/10-things-we-all-should-know-about-indigenous-people.

Chapter 15

1. Polyvagal Institute, "What is Polyvagal Theory?" *Polyvagal Institute*, accessed April 25, 2025, https://www.polyvagalinstitute.org/whatispolyvagaltheory.

2. Susan Fishman, "Can You Physically Feel Emotions?" *Psych Central*, July 21, 2022, https://psychcentral.com/blog/emotions-are-physical.

3. "Repressed Emotions: Symptoms, Causes, and Release," *Medical News Today*, accessed October 4, 2023, https://www.medicalnewstoday.com/articles/repressed-emotions.

4. Heal Thy Self w/ Dr. G, "How to Fast More Effectively," *YouTube*, May 7, 2024, https://www.youtube.com/watch?v=PIEg3euJsbM.

5. Gabor Maté, *When the Body Says No: Exploring the Stress-Disease Connection* (London: Vermilion, 2019), 173.

6. Doc Snipes, "What is the HPA Axis AKA The Stress Response," *YouTube*, Aug 19, 2022, https://www.youtube.com/watch?v=zrE9a9ouCGk

7. Gabor Maté, *When the Body Says No: Exploring the Stress-Disease Connection* (London: Vermilion, 2019), 7.

8. Mark Hyman, MD, "10 Steps to Reverse Autoimmune Disease," *YouTube*, Sep 3, 2015, https://www.youtube.com/watch?v=9Imp8iztaJc

9. Bessel van der Kolk, *The Body Keeps the Score: Brain, Mind, and Body in the Healing of Trauma* (New York: Viking, 2014), 66, 91.

10. Danielle Carr, "How Trauma Became America's Favorite Diagnosis," *New York Magazine*, July 31, 2023, https://nymag.com/intelligencer/article/trauma-bessel-van-der-kolk-the-body-keeps-the-score-profile.html.

11. Somatic Experiencing International, Nature's Lessons in Healing Trauma: An Introduction to Somatic Experiencing® (SE), YouTube, Oct 15, 2014, https://www.youtube.com/watch?v=nmJDkzDMllc.

12. Marie Kuhfuß *et al.*, "Somatic Experiencing: Effectiveness and Key Factors of a Body-Oriented Trauma Therapy—a Scoping Literature Review," *European Journal of Psychotraumatology* 12, no. 1 (2021): 1929023, https://doi.org/10.1080/20008198.2021.1929023.

Feldenkrais Guild of North America, "Home," *Feldenkrais Method*, February 10, 2025, https://feldenkrais.com/.

13. The Minded Institute, "Yoga for Chronic Pain," *The Minded Institute*, n.d., accessed April 25, 2025, https://themindedinstitute.com/yoga-for-chronic-pain/.

Chapter 16

1. Jack Kornfield, "The Mind and the Heart," *Jack Kornfield*, September 16, 2014, https://jackkornfield.com/mind-heart/.

2. Thomas R. Verny, M.D., "Intuition: What It Is and How It Works," *Psychology Today*, August 22, 2023, https://www.psychologytoday.com/us/blog/explorations-of-the-mind/202308/intuition-what-it-is-and-how-it-works.

3. Ted L. Tewfik, MD, "Vagus Nerve Anatomy," *eMedicine* (Medscape), updated February 20, 2025, https://emedicine.medscape.com/article/1875813-overview.

4. BrainFacts.Org, "Trust your Gut: How the Brain-Gut Connection Helps Us Decide Intuitively," YouTube, Sep 30, 2021, https://www.youtube.com/watch?v=sAo2FauXJDA&t=8s.

5. Joel Pearson, *The Intuition Toolkit: The New Science of Knowing What without Knowing Why* (New York: Simon & Schuster, 2024).

6. Science and Nonduality, "Connecting with the Intuitive Guidance of the Heart," YouTube, Feb 2, 2017, https://www.youtube.com/watch?v=apK8h1B9UbQ.

7. Cleveland Clinic. "Heart Rate Variability (HRV)." *Cleveland Clinic*. Last modified June 22, 2022. https://my.clevelandclinic.org/health/symptoms/21773-heart-rate-variability-hrv.

8. Xianghong Arakaki et al., "The Connection Between Heart Rate Variability (HRV), Neurological Health, and Cognition: A Literature Review," *Frontiers in Neuroscience*

17 (March 1, 2023): 1055445, https://doi.org/10.3389/
fnins.2023.1055445.

Chapter 17

1. Rupert Spira, "How You Create Time and Space in Your Own
   Mind," YouTube, Jun 16, 2023, https://www.youtube.com/
   watch?v=omZA2BJLtJA.

2. "10 Facts You Don't Know About Salvador Dali's 'Persistence
   of Memory'." *DaliPaintings.com.* Accessed April 26, 2025.
   https://www.dalipaintings.com/persistence-of-memory.jsp.

3. Charlie Wood, "What Is String Theory?" *Space.com*, accessed
   April 26, 2025. https://www.space.com/17594-string-theory.
   html.

4. Engineering Made Easy, "11 Dimensions Explained - A Mind-
   Bending Explanation of Higher Dimensions!" YouTube, May
   18, 2021, https://www.youtube.com/watch?v=UxubeeSqSmk.

5. Tereza Pultarova, "The Theory of Everything: Searching
   for the Universal Rules of Physics," *Space.com*, December
   18, 2022, https://www.space.com/theory-of-everything-
   definition.html.

6. Centre for Theoretical Cosmology. "The Origins of the
   Universe: M-theory." *Centre for Theoretical Cosmology.*
   Accessed April 26, 2025. https://www.ctc.cam.ac.uk/
   outreach/origins/quantum_cosmology_four.php.

Chapter 18

1. The Metropolitan Museum of Art. "Shiva as Lord of
   Dance (Nataraja)." Accessed April 26, 2025. https://www.
   metmuseum.org/art/collection/search/39328.

2. Istanbul Dervish Ceremony. "What Is a Whirling Dervish
   and Why Is It Called That?" Last modified March 7, 2021.
   https://istanbuldervishceremony.com/what-is-a-whirlin
   g-dervish-and-why-is-it-called-that/.

3. Ksenia Parkhatskaya, "Exploring the Spiritual Dimensions of Dance," *Secrets of Solo*, April 30, 2023, https://secretsofsolo.com/2023/04/spiritual-dimensions-of-dance/.

4. Piotr Gronek et al., "Is Dance Closer to Physical Activity or Spirituality? A Philosophical Exploration," *Journal of Religion and Health* 62, no. 2 (2023): 1314-1323, https://doi.org/10.1007/s10943-021-01354-y.

5. Abi Berger, "Magnetic Resonance Imaging," *BMJ* (Clinical Research Ed.) 324, no. 7328 (2002): 35, https://doi.org/10.1136/bmj.324.7328.35.

6. Donna Eden and David Feinstein, "Development of a Healthcare Approach Focusing on Subtle Energies: The Case of Eden Energy Medicine," *Advances in Mind-Body Medicine* 34, no. 3 (Summer 2020): 25–36, https://advances-journal.com/wp-content/uploads/2020/09/Eden.pdf.

7. Jessica Migala, "What Is Tai Chi? A Beginner's Guide to This Mind-Body Practice," *Everyday Health*, November 22, 2022, https://www.everydayhealth.com/wellness/tai-chi/guide/.

Chapter 19

1. World Freerunning Parkour Federation. "What Is Parkour?" *WFPF*. Accessed April 26, 2025. https://wfpf.com/parkour/.

2. Celia A. Brownell et al., '"So Big": The Development of Body Self-Awareness in Toddlers,' *Child Development* 78, no. 5 (2007): 1426–1440, https://doi.org/10.1111/j.1467-8624.2007.01075.x.

3. F. Diane Barth, "Dance Is a Powerful Tool for Emotional and Physical Health," *Psychology Today*, July 4, 2023, https://www.psychologytoday.com/us/blog/off-the-couch/202307/dance-is-a-powerful-tool-for-emotional-and-physical-health.

4. Ruthann Richter, "Dance for Parkinson's Disease at the Stanford Neuroscience Health Center," *Stanford Medicine*

Magazine, February 17, 2017, https://stanmed.stanford.edu/dance-for-parkinsons-disease-at-the-stanford-neuroscience-health-center/.

5. Daniel Aldana-Benítez, María José Caicedo-Pareja, Diana Patricia Sánchez, and Leidy Tatiana Ordoñez-Mora, "Dance as a Neurorehabilitation Strategy: A Systematic Review," *Journal of Bodywork and Movement Therapies* 35 (2023): 348–363, https://doi.org/10.1016/j.jbmt.2023.04.046.

6. Kira M. Newman, "Four Ways Dancing Makes You Happier," *Greater Good Magazine*, July 6, 2022, https://greatergood.berkeley.edu/article/item/four_ways_dancing_makes_you_happier.

7. Gaia Herbs, "A Guide to Traditional Herbalism Across Cultures," *Gaia Herbs*, April 15, 2024, https://www.gaiaherbs.com/blogs/seeds-of-knowledge/herbalism-folk-medicine.

Chapter 20

1. Maharishi International University. "Maharishi Effect." *Maharishi International University*, accessed April 26, 2025. https://research.miu.edu/maharishi-effect/.

2. Robert Krulwich, "Can a Plant Remember? This One Seems to—Here's the Evidence," *National Geographic*, December 15, 2015, https://www.nationalgeographic.com/science/article/can-a-plant-remember-this-one-seems-to-heres-the-evidence.

3. Richard Pallardy, "Which Animals Can Recognize Themselves in the Mirror?" *Live Science*, June 28, 2024, https://www.livescience.com/animals/which-animals-can-recognize-themselves-in-the-mirror.

4. Philip Goff, "Science as We Know It Can't Explain Consciousness – But a Revolution Is Coming," *The Conversation*, November 1, 2019, https://theconversation.com/science-as-we-know-it-cant-explain-consciousness-but-a-revolution-is-coming-126143.

5. Patricia MacCormack, "Animal consciousness: why it's time to rethink our human-centred approach" *The Conversation*, April 18, 2023, https://www.theguardian.com/commentisfree/article/2024/sep/07/when-dogs-recall-toys-and-horses-plan-ahead-are-animals-so-different-from-us.

6. TED-Ed, "How do animals experience pain?," YouTube, Jan 17, 2017, https://www.youtube.com/watch?v=5j9Syov0AAw.

7. Paula Droege et al., "Fishnition: Developing Models From Cognition Toward Consciousness," *Frontiers in Veterinary Science* 8 (2021): 785256, https://doi.org/10.3389/fvets.2021.785256.

8. "10 Things to Know About the Mycelial Network," *Fantastic Fungi*, October 5, 2022, https://fantasticfungi.com/blogs/news/10-things-to-know-about-the-mycelial-network.

9. Richard Grant, "Do Trees Talk to Each Other?" *Smithsonian Magazine*, March 2018, https://www.smithsonianmag.com/science-nature/the-whispering-trees-180968084/.

10. National Park Service, "Coast Redwood," *U.S. National Park Service*, last modified June 3, 2021, https://www.nps.gov/articles/000/coast-redwood.htm.

11. James Hurd Nixon, "Planetary Consciousness," *Planetary Philosophy*, https://www.planetaryphilosophy.com/2016/03/planetary-consciousness/.

Chapter 21

1. don Miguel Ruiz, The Four Agreements: A Practical Guide to Personal Freedom (San Rafael: Amber-Allen Publishing, 1997).

2. Dan Witters, "U.S. Depression Rates Reach New Highs," *Gallup News*, May 17, 2023, https://news.gallup.com/poll/505745/depression-rates-reach-new-highs.aspx.

3. Anxiety and Depression Association of America, "Anxiety Disorders – Facts & Statistics," accessed April 26, 2025, https://adaa.org/understanding-anxiety/facts-statistics.

4. Pew Research Center, "8 in 10 Americans Say Religion Is Losing Influence in Public Life," March 15, 2024, https://www.pewresearch.org/religion/2024/03/15/8-in-10-americans-say-religion-is-losing-influence-in-public-life/.

5. American Psychiatric Association, "New APA Poll: One in Three Americans Feels Lonely Every Week," January 30, 2024, https://www.psychiatry.org/news-room/news-releases/new-apa-poll-one-in-three-americans-feels-lonely-e.

6. Traci Pedersen, "Understanding Spiritual Depression," *Psych Central*, January 29, 2024, https://psychcentral.com/depression/spiritual-depression.

7. Dr. Laura Gabayan, *lauragabayan.com*, accessed April 27, 2025, https://lauragabayan.com/.

About the Author

Smita started her career as an engineer, jumping into software, technology, and start-ups in the early days of internet commerce. She enjoyed being a part of the evolution of the internet and artificial intelligence. Smita's life took a sharp turn when she had to grapple with complex chronic illness and found minimal help from mainstream medicine to feel better and heal. That began her years of experimentation with and research of alternative healing and holistic medicine. She realized that she owned her own health and wellbeing and there was an entirely different paradigm of health than what was presented in the mainstream practice of healthcare. She learned how to incorporate these modalities and improve her health. Smita even became a certified functional medicine health coach so she could help others in their health and wellbeing journeys. She decided to put her learnings in this book, *The Aligned Human*.

Thank You For Reading My Book!

I really appreciate all of your feedback and

I love hearing what you have to say.

I need your input to make the next version of this

Please take two minutes now to leave a helpful review on

Amazon letting me know what you thought of the book.

Thanks so much!

Smita

www.ingramcontent.com/pod-product-compliance
Lightning Source LLC
Chambersburg PA
CBHW060904120626
46553CB00001B/194